AFP SciTech Futures

AFPで学ぶ世界の科学

Atsushi Mukuhira
Bill Benfield
Tomoko Tsujimoto
Seiko Otsuka
Kazuya Kurazono
Hiroki Takikawa
Mariko Yuasa
Keiko Matsumoto

Streaming Materials

StreamLine

Web 動画・音声ファイルのストリーミング再生について

CD マーク及び Web 動画マークがある箇所は、PC、スマートフォン、タブレット端末において、無料でストリーミング再生することができます。下記 URL よりご利用ください。再生手順や動作環境などは本書巻末の「Web 動画のご案内」をご覧ください。

http://st.seibido.co.jp

音声ファイルのダウンロードについて

CD マークがある箇所は、ダウンロードすることも可能です。下記 URL の書籍詳細ページにあるダウンロードアイコンをクリックしてください。

http://seibido.co.jp/ad604

AFP SciTech Futures

はじめに

　いやおうなく、世界は変容します。地球温暖化による気候変動や、グローバリズムの進展による政治・経済の混迷、そして2020年の新型コロナ禍など、人類や地球上の環境・生態系すべてに突きつけられる局面は、刻々と激しく揺れ動きます。そして、そのすべての場面で必ず登場し関与するのが、科学であり、工学です。サイエンスやテクノロジーは、世界の行く末がかすむ方向に変容する破壊的要因にもなりますし、また一方で、未来に一筋の光が差すための頼もしい礎となり、道具にもなります。人類が手にする科学・技術の潜在力を、そのどちらの方向に用いるのか ― それが、今回生まれて初めて世界規模の"有事"を経験し、未来への欲求をこれまでになく募らせた現代を生きる私たちの、喫緊の課題です。

　本書AFP SciTech Futuresの素材は、フランスを拠点としてさまざまな言語でニュースを配信しているAFP通信が、今を生きる私たちにとって利用価値の高い動画・画像をストックしている「保管庫」AFP World Academic Archiveです。本書は、その多量のストックの中から世界中の科学・技術に関する20の最新映像ニュースを選りすぐり、教材化したものです。どの映像にも、科学や工学のきわどい両義性や、より複雑に入り組んだ人間社会の精神性が織り込まれています。皆さんがこれらのニュース素材と教材に触れながら、単に科学・技術関係の英語運用力だけでなく、現実社会でよりリアルに生き抜く対応力を開拓してもらえることを、著者一同期待しています。

　本書の作成にあたっては、株式会社成美堂の工藤隆志氏に大変お世話になりました。暗闇の中で足取りのおぼつかない本書の著者陣に根気強い支援を与えてくださった氏に、心からの感謝を記したいと思います。

2020年　秋

著者一同

本書の構成・使い方

VOCABULARY

A. ニュース・スクリプトで使われている5つの語彙の意味を確認します。

B. ニュース・スクリプトに出てくる3つのフレーズを取り上げ、その意味を把握するとともに、ある音（ほとんどの場合は母音）についての発音を確認します。この作業によって音声面に目を向け、ニュースの音声に対する聴解力を高めます。

FINDING THE TOPIC

ニュースを一度視聴し、話題・内容と流れをごく簡単に把握しておくセクションです。

CHECKING THE SCRIPT

再度ニュースの音声を聴いて、空所に入る語（すべて1語）を書き取ります。この空所に入る語はすべてVocabularyで取り上げた語彙が入るので、スペリングが不明の時はVocabularyを参照してください。ただし、名詞の単複や動詞の形などを変更する必要がある場合もあります。

空所が埋められたら、ニュース・スクリプトの内容をさらに深く把握しましょう。

なお、［　　］の挿入部は著者による修正です。

［→ ×］：文法や内容的に直前の語句が不要な場合

［→ 別の語句］：文法や内容的に誤った語句を差し替える場合

［語句］：文法的に必要な語句を追加する場合

COMPREHENSION

ニュース・スクリプトの内容に関する理解度チェックの問題です。

PRESENTING THE CONTENTS

ニュース・スクリプトの要点を、プレゼンテーションのスピーチ形式にまとめたものです。音声を聴いて空所に入る語（すべて1語）を書き取りましょう。あるいは、空所に入る語は原則的にスクリプトに出てきた語彙なので、音声を聴かないでスピーチの内容を把握し、入れるべき語を推測する方法も有効です。時間に余裕があれば、スピーチの内容を正確に把握したり、聴衆に向けてスピーチの練習をしてみることも良いでしょう。さらに、使用されている構文や表現の多くは実際のプレゼンに活用できるものなので、プレゼン原稿を作成する機会などに利用しましょう。

PINPOINT

科学・技術の諸分野で頻出する語彙・語法・表現などを取り上げ、簡単な解説と練習問題を提供するセクションです。

FURTHER INVESTIGATION

科学・技術の諸分野で頻出する文書形式・図版やレイアウトに注目して問題に解答したり、専門的語彙に慣れるためのセクションです。いずれも科学・技術系ESPにとっては重要な情報なので、確実にマスターしておきましょう。

* スペリングについて

AFP通信は基本的に英国式スペリングを採用しているため、本書でも原則としてそれに従っています。ただし、米国のニュースを扱うUnitでは米国式を採用しています。

Contents

Protecting Communities and History

Future of the Earth and Universe

Dissolving Bags

キャッサバが救う危機

プラスチックによる海洋汚染が、海の生物の生息環境を脅かしています。レジ袋やストローなど、日常生活で多用されるプラスチックに取って代わる素材として注目されるのが、生育力豊かなキャッサバ。タピオカの原料でもあるこの熱帯低木は、世界のプラ汚染を改善する "スィート" な切り札になりえるでしょうか。

VOCABULARY 🎧 CD 1-03

A 次の語句に対応する日本語を選びましょう。

1. dissolve （　）
2. tropical root （　）
3. diverse （　）
4. discard （　）
5. sea animal （　）

a. 多様な
b. 廃棄する
c. 海洋動物
d. 熱帯植物の根
e. 溶けて無くなる

B 次の語句の下線部と同じ発音が含まれる語を、Aの語句から1つずつ選びましょう。

1. mar<u>i</u>ne littering 「海へのポイ捨て」 （　）

2. b<u>io</u>degradable product 「生分解性製品」 （　）
   （細菌作用によって無害な物質へと分解される製品）

3. artificial counterp<u>ar</u>t 「（キャッサバ製ではない）人工的な製品」 （　）

FINDING THE TOPIC 🖥 WEB動画 💿 DVD

次の英文が映像の内容と合っている場合はTを、合っていない場合はFを選びましょう。

1. Apart from China, Indonesia is the world's largest producer of marine littering. T / F

2. Even though cassava bags are more expensive than plastic ones, Indonesian consumers prefer them. T / F

3. Indonesia's government does not make money available to combat the problem of plastic waste. T / F

● *CHECKING THE SCRIPT*

WEB動画 DVD CD 1-04

A 音声を聴いて、空所に入る語を書き取りましょう。
B スクリプトを読んで、内容を把握しましょう。

Kevin Kumala: co-founder of Avani Eco

Tuti Hendrawati Mintarsih: Director General for solid waste at the Indonesian
Ministry of the Environment

Narrator: You can burn it. You can even drink it. This carrier
bag was not made with plastic, but with cassava,
a ¹(   ) root found abundantly in
Indonesia.

abundantly 豊富に

Kevin Kumala: Our bags are so eco-friendly that it has passed   5
oral toxicity tests, in which it is totally harmless for
animals to consume it. So, me drinking it is just to
show you that this is so harmless, and it gives you
hope for these sea ²(   ).

oral toxicity test
経口毒性試験

Narrator: Indonesia is facing a plastic waste crisis driven by   10
years of economic growth in one of the world's most
³(   ) ecosystems. When it comes
to ⁴(   ) littering, the archipelago
of over 17,000 islands is the world's number two,
after China, according to a study.   15

ecosystem 生態系

archipelago 群島

Kevin Kumala: Just in Indonesia alone, a country of a
population of 255 million people, if you're talking
about straws alone, we're talking about 255 million
people times 20 centimetres of plastic straw being
⁵(   ) every single day. That is   20
5,000 kilometres of plastic being discarded on a
daily basis, and that is equivalent [to] the distance
of Jakarta to Sydney.

on a daily basis 毎日
equivalent to... 〜に相
当する

Narrator: Unlike the years needed for conventional plastic,
most of these biodegradable ⁶(   )   25
can break down in just a few months. But it all
comes at a price. A cassava bag costs nearly twice
the price of its artificial counterpart, which so far

break down 分解される

come at a price 高くつく

2

has deterred consumers in Southeast Asia's largest market.

30

deter 思いとどまらせる

Tuti Hendrawati Mintarsih: But, if the market in Indonesia increase [→increases], and [→×] then they will increase the production for Indonesian [→Indonesians], and also the price of the plastic [→cassava] bag also will be cheaper.

35

Narrator: Indonesia currently has no government funding aimed at reducing plastic waste. But, despite many challenges, the hopes of its small bio-producers are unlikely to easily ⁷( ).

government funding
政府の財政援助

● *COMPREHENSION*

1 については質問に対する答えを、2 については下線部に入るものを選びましょう。

1. What is NOT true of bags made from cassava root?
   (A) They are biodegradable.
   (B) They cost more than plastic bags.
   (C) They are a best-selling item in Southeast Asia.
   (D) They are not poisonous.

2. After several years of high economic growth, Indonesia is _____ a plastic waste crisis.
   (A) facing
   (B) meeting
   (C) breaking
   (D) preparing

● PRESENTING THE CONTENTS

CD 1-05

次の英文は、スクリプトの要点をプレゼンテーションのスピーチ形式にまとめたものです。
音声を聴いて、空所に入る語句を記入しましょう。

The world is facing a 1)_____ of plastic waste, which is growing daily. The situation in Indonesia is serious, but the country has devised an innovative solution. After China, Indonesia is the world's largest producer of plastic waste that ends up in the sea. Estimates put the combined length of the plastic straws 2)_____ daily in the country at 5,000 kilometres. One company has come up with a new idea to 3)_____ the use of plastic bags. Instead of plastic, it uses cassava, a root that grows abundantly in the country. It has two main advantages. First, it is 4)_____ and breaks down quickly. Second, it is not poisonous and will not harm animals. Unfortunately, cassava bags are twice the price of plastic bags, but if the market for them increases, their price will come down.

● PINPOINT

「順位」を表す表現には次のようなものがあります。日本語を参考にして、英語の空所に入る語を枠内から選びましょう。

1. The population of Indonesia _____ fourth in the world.
    「インドネシアの人口は世界第4位です。」

2. The area of Indonesia's Java Island is _____ to that of Sumatra Island.
    「インドネシアのジャワ島の面積は、スマトラ島の面積に次いでいます。」

3. China's economy is the second largest in the world _____ that of the US.
    「中国の経済は、米国に次いで世界で2番目に大きいです。」

4. Regarding the amount of marine littering, China is the world's _____ one.
    「海へのポイ捨ての量については、中国が世界第1位です。」

number	next	ranks	after

4

FURTHER INVESTIGATION

表（table）は、データを一覧にまとめることによって特徴や傾向を明確にする情報整理の手段です。ランキング表（ranking table）として、特定の視点で順位づけるものもあります。

次のランキング表は、世界における 2017 年のキャッサバ生産量の作付面積と順位を一覧にしたものです。下記の英文の空所に入る適切な国名を記入しましょう。

Rank	Country	Production (million tonne)	Area harvested (million hectare)
1	Nigeria	59.49	6.79
2	Congo	31.60	0.14
3	Thailand	30.97	1.34
4	Indonesia	19.05	0.78
5	Brazil	18.88	1.31
6	Ghana	18.47	0.97
7	Angola	11.75	1.01
8	Cambodia	10.58	0.39
9	Viet Nam	10.27	0.53
10	Mozambique	8.77	1.07

(Based on: The Food and Agriculture Organization of the United Nations)

1. In the world, _____ ranked first in both the production of cassava and the area harvested in 2017.

2. The table shows that _____ had the largest cassava production among Asian countries.

3. With regard to the area harvested, _____ was the third largest after Nigeria and Thailand.

4. The area harvested in _____ was next to that in Ghana.

Farm beneath the Streets

地下で地産地消

世界有数の大都市、ロンドン。その地下に、思いもよらない緑の野菜畑が広がりつつあります。収穫されるのは、生育環境を効率的に管理されたマイクログリーン（micro green）。ブロッコリーやルッコラなど、栄養価の高い新鮮 "地場野菜" は、世界的食糧難が危惧される未来を救う栄養源となりますかどうか…。

VOCABULARY
🔊 1-07

A 次の語句に対応する日本語を選びましょう。

1. nutrient-rich　　（　　）
2. cultivate　　　　（　　）
3. grapple　　　　（　　）
4. sprout　　　　　（　　）
5. farm equipment（　　）

a. 発芽させる
b. 農業設備
c. 取り組む
d. 栽培する
e. 栄養豊富な

B 次の語句の下線部と同じ発音が含まれる語を、A の語句から 1 つずつ選びましょう。

1. air-r<u>ai</u>d shelter 「防空壕」　　　　　　　　　　　　　　　（　　）

2. controlled-environment <u>a</u>griculture 「環境制御農業」
（作物の生育環境を制御して生産効率を上げる農業）　　　　　　　（　　）

3. ren<u>ew</u>able energy source 「再生エネルギー源」　　　　　　（　　）

FINDING THE TOPIC
WEB動画　DVD

次の英文が映像の内容と合っている場合は T を、合っていない場合は F を選びましょう。

1. The producers take advantage of low electricity prices during nighttime hours.　　　　　　　　　　　　　　　　　　T / F

2. One great advantage of underground farming is the ability to closely control the growing environment.　　　　　　　　　T / F

3. The prominent UK supermarket Marks & Spencer is considering selling produce from the underground farm.　　　　　　T / F

CHECKING THE SCRIPT

WEB動画 DVD CD 1-08

A 音声を聴いて、空所に入る語を書き取りましょう。
B スクリプトを読んで、内容を把握しましょう。

Steven Dring: co-founder of Growing Underground
Charlie Curtis: agronomist at Marks & Spencer

Narrator: Thirty-three metres below south London is not where you'd expect to find a farm. But two years ago, this former air-raid ¹( ) began to sprout rocket, coriander and even broccoli. Instead of using soil and natural light, the ⁵ plants grow thanks to LEDs and hydroponics using ²( ) water.

former かつての
rocket ルッコラ
coriander コリアンダー

hydrophonics 水耕栽培

Steven Dring: Because we are in what is called controlled-environment ³( ), we have a lot more control than usual growers. So, we manage to ₁₀ negate a lot of those challenges by the fact that we can control the humidity, we can control the heat. But there's nothing that stands out, that I would say is a major challenge, apart from building a farm underneath London. ₁₅

negate 無効にする
challenge 難題
stand out 際立つ

Narrator: All of the electricity comes from renewable energy ⁴( ), and the LEDs shine brightest at night when electricity is cheapest. And the farm has managed to bag some top-shelf clients, including supermarket chain Marks & Spencer. ₂₀

bag 獲得する
top-shelf 一流の
Marks & Spencer マークス＆スペンサー（英国の小売業者）

Charlie Curtis: I think the story is fantastic. I think we all love to think that our food is grown locally to us. And, but I think also the product sells itself. The quality is fantastic, and the taste, and the flavour is like something I've never had before. It's brilliant. ₂₅

Narrator: Currently around a dozen micro greens and salads are ⁵( ) here. And there's still room for new growth.

sell itself 放っておいても売れる

Steven Dring: So, this is what the tunnel looks like before we start to put the farm [6]( ) in here. 30 So, as you've seen, we've given it a food-safe lining, we've painted the floors. And then, what this does, it gives us an additional storage capacity, so we start to expand and start to fulfill that customer demand that's out there. 35

Narrator: The farm's founders say this type of farming is 100 times cheaper than overground urban farming. Not being at the mercy of British weather means a more reliable crop. And, as the world [7]( ) with climate change and a 40 rapidly growing population, experts say farms like these could be the answer.

food-safe lining 食物が安全
な内張り
storage capacity （市場に
供給するための）生産スペース
at the mercy of... ～に左右
される

● COMPREHENSION

質問に対する答えを選びましょう。

1. What method is used to grow the vegetables?
   (A) Hydroelectricity
   (B) Hydrogen
   (C) Hydrotherapy
   (D) Hydroponics

2. What does the Marks & Spencer employee mention about the produce from the underground farm?
   (A) Its colour
   (B) Its price
   (C) Its variety
   (D) Its taste

PRESENTING THE CONTENTS

 1-09

次の英文は、スクリプトの要点をプレゼンテーションのスピーチ形式にまとめたものです。
音声を聴いて、空所に入る語句を記入しましょう。

When it comes to maintaining an adequate food supply, there are two important factors: worsening climate change and the continued growth of the global 1)_____. To avoid food shortages, it is vital to consider alternative forms of agriculture. One innovative idea is to grow crops underground. One advantage of this approach is that the growing environment can be completely 2)_____. Another is that the crops are not at the 3)_____ of unpredictable weather. A company in London has recently set up such an operation using an old air-raid 4)_____. The venture has been a success. Not only is the produce cheaper than crops grown above ground, its vegetables have won praise for their flavour and high quality. Some major UK supermarket chains are already stocking the produce.

PINPOINT

関係副詞は、先行する名詞（句）が無くても名詞節を作ることができます。

（例）The underground below London is not (a place) <u>where</u> you would expect to find a farm.
「ロンドンの地下は、農場を見つけることが期待できるような場所ではありません。」

日本語を参考にして、英文の空所に入る適切な語を枠内から選びましょう。

1. I remember _____ I first got into the tunnel under the ground.
   「私は、地下のトンネルに初めて入ったときのことを覚えています。」

2. This is _____ the underground vegetables sell themselves.
   「これが、地下で栽培された野菜が放っておいても売れる理由です。」

3. On its website, the company shows _____ they will reduce CO_2 emissions in London.
   「この企業はウェブサイトで、ロンドンでのCO2排出をどのように削減しようとしているかを紹介しています。」

how	when	why

FURTHER INVESTIGATION

> プロセスチャート（工程図）は、文字情報を分かりやすく補足するだけでなく、視覚に訴えることで情報のインパクトを増幅する効果があります。

次の工程図は、水耕栽培の一種であるエアロポニックス（aeroponics）の仕組みを説明したものです。図を参考に、英文の空所に入る適切な語を下記から選びましょう。

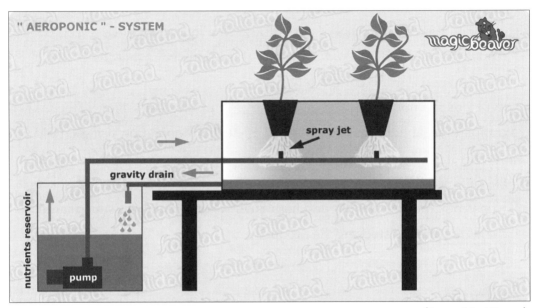

(Source: MagicBeaver)

How the Aeroponic System Works

1. A certain amount of the (　　) solution is stored in the reservoir.

2. The water (　　) delivers the solution through the pipe.

3. The solution is sprayed from the (　　) nozzles.

4. The (　　) of plants suspended in the box absorb the sprayed solution.

5. The surplus water falls down from the gravity drain to the (　　).

a. reservoir	b. pump	c. jet	d. nutrient	e. roots

Mechanics are Men —
Think Again!

ジェンダー・フリーな車整備

女性は機械が苦手—これも一種の固定観念です。男性の仕事として認識されてきた自動車整備に、自ら名乗りを上げる女性たちがいます。ネイルサロン併設の彼女らの店に、親近感を抱く女性客が多数来店することで、自動車整備業界に風穴が開くかもしれません。なんせ、米国の運転免許所有者の約半数は女性ですから。

VOCABULARY

CD 1-11

A 次の語句に対応する日本語を選びましょう。

1. vehicle   (   )   a. 権限を与える
2. garage   (   )   b. 車両
3. empower   (   )   c. おびえさせる
4. airhead   (   )   d. 能無し
5. intimidate   (   )   e. 自動車修理店

B 次の語句の下線部と同じ発音が含まれる語を、A の語句から 1 つずつ選びましょう。

1. car rep<u>air</u> shop 「自動車修理店」   (   )

2. "sh<u>e</u>canic" 「シーカニック」（自動車修理を苦手としない女性整備士を指す造語）   (   )

3. n<u>a</u>tionwide franchise 「全国的なフランチャイズ」   (   )

FINDING THE TOPIC

WEB動画
DVD

次の英文が映像の内容と合っている場合は T を、合っていない場合は F を選びましょう。

1. All the staff members of Patrice Banks's car repair shop are women.   T / F

2. Patrice Banks's shop also offers a manicure service.   T / F

3. Fewer than 10 percent of car technicians and mechanics in the U.S. are   T / F
   women.

● *CHECKING THE SCRIPT*

A 音声を聴いて、空所に入る語を書き取りましょう。
B スクリプトを読んで、内容を把握しましょう。

Patrice Banks: founder and CEO of Girls Auto Clinic

Sue Sweeney: mechanic, forewoman of Girls Auto Clinic

Tenny Agustin: Girls Auto Clinic customer

Narrator: Patrice Banks used to manage an engineering lab, before switching gears. Now she runs Girls Auto Clinic, an almost all-female car repair shop outside of Philadelphia.

Patrice Banks: We show women how to take these and clean 5 them.

switch gear 仕事を変える

Narrator: Patrice used to dread routine car checkups, ¹( ) by an industry that caters mostly to men. Unable to find a female mechanic, she decided to take things into her own hands and 10 become one herself.

dread 恐れる
routine car checkup 車の定期点検
cater to... ～を対象とする
take...into one's own hands 自分の手で～を何とかする

Patrice Banks: Millions of other women, too, just like me, feel taken advantage of [as] auto ²( ), hate their experiences, need a guy, got to call their husband. It's not a very ³( ) 15 space to be in. We usually just accept our auto airhead fate right well, "This is kind of how it is," and now you don't have to do that anymore.

Narrator: After completing her training, she began hosting a series of workshops to educate other women about 20 their cars. They were so successful she opened up her own ⁴( ) complete with a nail salon for customers. Just over a year old, Girls Auto Clinic employs 10 people, nine of which are women. They call themselves "⁵( )," and 25 many say the shop means an end to stereotypes they have faced throughout their careers.

complete with... ～を備えた

Sue Sweeney: I can come in, be me, I can dress however I want, per se. I'm not going to get judged whether I look girlie enough or too boyish, per se, because of the 30 type of work I'm going to do that day.

per se まあ、いわば

Narrator: Women make up nearly half of all drivers in the U.S. But female technicians and mechanics total only about three percent. Patrice says the large majority of her customers are female. 35

Tenny Agustin: Yeah, I think it's definitely worth a 30-minute trip because it's a lot more intimate of an experience and I get to really learn more about my ⁶( ).

intimate 親密な

Narrator: Girls Auto Clinic is looking to capitalize on its 40 loyal customer base. They have just launched a crowdfunding campaign with the goal of hiring "shecanics" across the country and turning the shop into a nationwide ⁷( ).

capitalize on... ～を最大活用する
loyal customer 上顧客

COMPREHENSION

1 については質問に対する答えを、2 については下線部に入るものを選びましょう。

1. Why did Patrice Banks open up her own garage?
   (A) She lost her job as manager of an engineering lab.
   (B) Her nail salon went out of business.
   (C) She found a lot of female mechanics.
   (D) Her training workshops for women were successful.

2. Patrice banks felt that male mechanics took _____ of her and other women customers.
   (A) advantage
   (B) benefit
   (C) profit
   (D) money

次の英文は、スクリプトの要点をプレゼンテーションのスピーチ形式にまとめたものです。
音声を聴いて、空所に入る語句を記入しましょう。

Women entrepreneurs have been the focus of my research in recent years. Today, I will be talking about Patrice Banks. Patrice used to manage an engineering lab, but now she runs an almost all-female car repair shop. She used to 1)_____ car checkups because she thought male mechanics would take advantage of women customers. After training as an auto mechanic, she held 2)_____ to educate other women. They were so successful that she opened her own shop. Nearly half of the drivers in the U.S. are women, but female 3)_____ and mechanics make up only about three percent of the total. Patrice wants to 4)_____ a nationwide franchise and has launched a crowdfunding campaign with the goal of hiring "shechanics" across the country.

● **PINPOINT**

数量を示す語や具体的な数値の前に付いて「およそ〜、約〜、ほとんど〜、ほぼ〜」を示す副詞には以下のようなものがあります。ニュアンスが異なるので、用法に注意しましょう。

（例）・about「およそ〜、約〜」（超過／未満のどちらでも可）
　　　・approximately「およそ〜、約〜」（超過／未満のどちらでも可。aboutよりも
　　　　　　　　　　　　　　　　　　　　正式）
　　　・almost「ほとんど〜、ほぼ〜」（未満の場合のみ可）
　　　・nearly「ほとんど〜、ほぼ〜」（未満の場合のみ可。almostよりもさらに離れる）

日本語を参考にして、英語の空所に入る適切な語を枠内から選びましょう。

1.　an almost _____-female shop
　　　「ほとんど全員が女性店員の店」

2.　nearly _____ of all drivers in the U.S.
　　　「米国の全ドライバーのほぼ半分」

3.　_____ 185,000 technicians
　　　「およそ18万５千人の技術者」

all	approximately	half

FURTHER INVESTIGATION

棒グラフ（bar graph）は、複数の項目を同じ観点で比較する際に有効なチャートです。また、棒グラフにランキング情報を組み込むことも可能です（ranked bar graph）。

次のグラフは、米国女性が従事する人数を職業別に比較したものです。2つのグラフ（上段：2018 年、下段：2010 年）を比べて、内容と合っているものを下記の1～4から2つ選びましょう。

Top 10 Occupations Employing the Largest Number of Women (Upper: 2018, Lower: 2010)

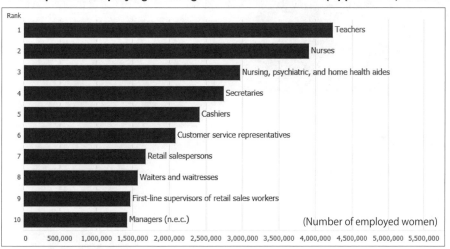

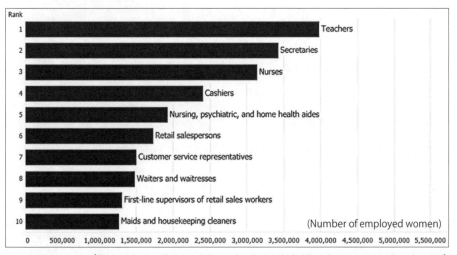

(Source: https://www.dol.gov/agencies/wb/data/occupations-decades-100)

1. More women worked as nurses in 2018 than in 2010.

2. The rank of secretaries went up from 2010 to 2018.

3. Housekeepers still ranked in the top 10 in 2018.

4. No occupation in engineering fields appears in either graph.

Pets Get High-class Health Care

ペット医療の最先端

平均寿命が延びているのは、なにも人間に限りません。犬や猫など、家庭のペットも近年は長寿化しているようです。大きな要因は、ペット医療の高度化。親愛なる家族の一員と長く過ごせるのは喜ばしいことですが、人間の治療と同じ方法で動物をケアすることは、場合によっては「猫に小判」の危険をはらむかも…。

VOCABULARY

🎵 CD 1-15

A 次の語句に対応する日本語を選びましょう。

1. companion （ ）
2. treat （ ）
3. medication （ ）
4. loose tooth （ ）
5. joint （ ）

a. 関節
b. ぐらぐらする歯
c. 治療する
d. 仲間
e. 薬

B 次の語句の下線部と同じ発音が含まれる語を、A の語句から 1 つずつ選びましょう。

1. hydro<u>th</u>erapy 「水治療法」 （ ）

2. one-to-one workout <u>se</u>ssion 「マンツーマン指導付きの運動セッション」 （ ）

3. humanization of domestic <u>a</u>nimals 「家庭にいる動物を人間のように扱うこと」

（ ）

FINDING THE TOPIC

WEB動画 🖥 🎵 DVD

次の英文が映像の内容と合っている場合は T を、合っていない場合は F を選びましょう。

1. Laser therapy is offered to dogs in place of giving them medication. T / F

2. Total spending on pets in the U.S. is expected to hit $3 billion this year. T / F

3. Owners are encouraged to ask for advice before treating their pets in a more human-like way. T / F

CHECKING THE SCRIPT

WEB動画 💻 / 📀 DVD / 💿 CD 1-16

A 音声を聴いて、空所に入る語を書き取りましょう。
B スクリプトを読んで、内容を把握しましょう。

Janay Austin Carlson: physiotherapist at Friendship Hospital for Animals

Freya Jackson: owner of dog Bella

Dr. Christine Klippen: veterinarian at Friendship Hospital for Animals

Dr. Brant Hassell: veterinarian at District Veterinary Hospital

Narrator: A full-grown house cat calmly wading through water might seem like an unusual sight, but it's all too common at this animal hospital in Washington, DC. Bess, an 11-year-old Maine Coon cat, is getting her weekly dose of ¹(   ) to help 5 with her arthritis. Another patient, Bella, is having laser therapy on her ²(   ) before she, too, will enter the hydro-tank.

full-grown 成長した
wade through... ～を歩く
Maine Coon メイン・クーン
　（猫の一種）
dose 決められた量
arthritis 関節炎
laser therapy レーザー治療
supplemental 補助的な
inflammation 炎症
discomfort 不快感

Janay Austin Carlson: So, it's sort of a supplemental treatment that can help us with that inflammation and 10 discomfort, and changes from the arthritis without having to take any ³(   ).

Narrator: With laser therapy costing $65 and hydrotherapy another $89 per session, these treatments aren't cheap, but pet owners say it's worth it. 15

Freya Jackson: I invest in myself to stay fit and healthy and able to run around, and why wouldn't I invest in my dog? It's a similar cost to, like, a one-to-one ⁴(   ) session for a human in a gym. And that to me seems perfectly reasonable. 20

invest in... ～に投資する

Narrator: Annual spending on pets has reached a record high of $72.5 billion in the U.S. and is expected to rise another $3 billion this year. It's part of a growing trend of humanization of domestic animals.

Dr. Christine Klippen: Our relationship with our pets is increasing, 25 and so with that, wanting to do what's best for our ⁵(   ) and those who are the patients that are part of our family has started to increase, even dramatically over the last 10 years.

Narrator: Younger pet owners are trending toward having pets before starting families, leaving them with more disposable income to spend on their furry friends, both for supplemental therapies like acupuncture and more basic healthcare like teeth cleaning.

30

35

trend toward... ～する傾向
がある
start a family 子どもを持つ
disposable 自由に使える
furry 毛がふさふさした
acupuncture 鍼治療
teeth cleaning 歯垢除去

Dr. Brant Hassell: These dogs are a lot of people's first children. So they really…if I say, "Oh, my goodness, this dog has a loose ⁶(   )," they're just like, "My baby!" and they want to take care of them.

40

Narrator: While there are many benefits, experts warn that in some cases ⁷(   ) animals like humans can pose health risks. They say owners should always seek guidance before imposing their own dietary or health regimens on their pets.

45

impose 無理に与える

dietary or health regimen
食事療法や健康療法

◗ COMPREHENSION

1 については質問に対する答えを、2 については下線部に入るものを選びましょう。

1. Which of the following treatments is NOT available for animals?
    (A) Hydrotherapy
    (B) Acupuncture
    (C) Laser therapy
    (D) One-to-one workouts

2. Pet owners say that the treatments are expensive, but they are _____ the high price.
    (A) value   (B) deserve   (C) worth   (D) suited

● PRESENTING THE CONTENTS 🎵 CD 1-17

次の英文は、スクリプトの要点をプレゼンテーションのスピーチ形式にまとめたものです。
音声を聴いて、空所に入る語句を記入しましょう。

In an animal hospital in Washington, DC, hydrotherapy and laser therapy are available for cats and dogs with arthritis. The treatments are expensive, but pet owners say it is worth it. Let's take a look at this chart. You can see that annual 1)_____ on pets in the U.S. has reached a record high of $72.5 billion and is expected to rise another $3 billion this year in a growing trend to humanize 2)_____ animals. Younger pet owners have pets before starting families, which means they have more 3)_____ income to spend on animal healthcare. However, experts warn that treating animals like humans can 4)_____ health risks. They say owners should seek guidance before imposing their own dietary or health regimens on their pets.

● PINPOINT

「with ＋ O（目的語）＋ C（補語）」を用いることで、「O が～しながら / ～なので」という意味を追加することができます（付帯状況）。補語にはしばしば現在分詞や過去分詞が入ります。

（例） With laser therapy costing $65 per session, the treatment is not cheap.
            O   C
「レーザー治療は1回につき65ドルの費用がかかるので、その治療は安くはありません。」

次の英文の（　　）内の動詞を適切な形に変えましょう。

1. With her body (brush →   ) gently by the trimmer, the dog looks very comfortable.

2. With the amount of investment in pets (rise →   ) dramatically over the years, pet owners still want to do what is best for their companions.

各種のアンケートや質問票（questionnaire）には、必要な情報を確実に回収する目的で、回答する側の負担を可能な限り軽減するためのさまざまな工夫が選択肢や回答欄に見られます。

次の枠内は、ある動物病院の問診票です。下記の１〜５が内容と合っている場合はＴを、合っていない場合はＦを記入しましょう。

SPUNKY ANIMAL HOSPITAL

Date:_____
Client name:_____
Pet's name:_____

◆Primary Reason for Today's Visit:_____

    Do you want your pet's nails to be trimmed today?: *Yes / No*
    For cats only: *Indoor / Outdoor / Both*
    Does your pet have a microchip?: *Yes / No*
    Do you feed your pet a raw meat diet?: *Yes / No*
    Do you give your pet human food?: *Yes / No*
    Type of food: *Canned / Dry / Both*   Brand:_____
    Is your pet taking any long-term prescriptions, over-the-counter drugs or herbal
    remedies?: *Yes / No*   If yes, what?:_____
    Does your pet have any known allergies to any medications?: *Yes / No*
    Does your pet have any chronic medical problems?: *Yes / No*
    Is your pet on flea control?: *Yes / No*   If yes, what kind?:_____

◆We would like to use cute pictures of our patients on our website or in our newsletters, but we do need your permission.
    I authorize the use of my pet's images on your websites or any social media and paper-based media.
    Signature:_____

1. (   ) 飼い主の名前は記入する必要がない。

2. (   ) ペットが犬の場合、室内犬かどうかを回答することが求められている。

3. (   ) 飼い主が自分で食べる食事をペットにも与えている場合、どのような物を与えているかについて回答することが求められている。

4. (   ) ペットが慢性的な病状を持っているかどうかについては、問われていない。

5. (   ) この動物病院では、治療したペットの写真をホームページに掲載することがある。

Life with the Iron Lady

花の都の老舗タワー

エッフェル塔は、第4回パリ万国博覧会（1889年）を機に建築されたランドマーク。観光客を魅了するロマンチックな品格と、堅固な鉄塔の組み合わせは、いつしか「鉄の貴婦人（The Iron Lady）」という愛称を生みました。その後も先端的な維持管理が施され、100年以上たった今日も優雅に花の都を見守ります。

VOCABULARY　🎵CD 1-19

Ａ 次の語句に対応する日本語を選びましょう。

1. spire （　）	a. 外部の塗装
2. summit （　）	b. 頂上
3. icon （　）	c. 尖塔
4. exterior paint （　）	d. 象徴
5. hydraulic （　）	e. 油圧式の

Ｂ 次の語句の下線部と同じ発音が含まれる語を、Aの語句から1つずつ選びましょう。

1. daily test r<u>u</u>n「日々の試験運行」 （　　）

2. turn-of-the-century <u>o</u>rigin
 「（19世紀から20世紀の）世紀の変わり目ごろの起源」 （　　）

3. f<u>ai</u>nt of heart「臆病な人」 （　　）

FINDING THE TOPIC　WEB動画 💻 📀DVD

次の英文が映像の内容と合っている場合はTを、合っていない場合はFを選びましょう。

1. The first elevators of the day in the Eiffel Tower are full of visitors.　T / F

2. Every 10 years, the elevator cables are changed and the tower is repainted.　T / F

3. The Eiffel Tower is a popular site for marriage proposals, especially in the evening.　T / F

CHECKING THE SCRIPT

WEB動画 📺 DVD 💿 CD 1-20

A 音声を聴いて、空所に入る語を書き取りましょう。
B スクリプトを読んで、内容を把握しましょう。

Henri-Claude Pellier: lift mechanic

Wilhem Dubelloy: tour guide

Jacques Barrière: chief electrician

Narrator: From its steampunk machine rooms to the lights and antennae at its peak, the Eiffel Tower with its 7,300 tons of iron is a moving, humming tourist centre that's been an ¹(   ) of the French capital for 128 years. The top is where everyone 5 wants to go, and for that, elevators are essential. But the first ones of the day go up completely empty. Henri-Claude, one of the elevator mechanics, is making the daily test ²(   ).

Henri-Claude Pellier: We have many sensors. We have a whole 10 lot of information coming in from all over the tower, and by monitoring these screens, we can know everything that's happening.

Narrator: Some of the elevators are still ³(   ), true to their turn-of-the-century origins. The 15 cables are regularly checked with ultrasound and completely changed every seven years, just like the ⁴(   ) paint. A ride in one of them is a chance to fly over Paris, but also to ask questions to guides like Wilhelm Dubelloy. After 20 10 years working on the tower, where marriage proposals are a daily occurrence, he's seen all kinds of ways of popping the question.

Wilhem Dubelloy: It once happened that the guy lost the ring. The lady was crying. He was not…he was extremely in 25 a [→×] bad shape. He…the ring…we never found the ring again.

steampunk
スチームパンク風の
machine room 機械室
humming 活気のある

elevator mechanics エレベーター整備士

true to... 〜のまま
ultrasound 超音波

daily occurrence 毎日起きること
pop the question 結婚を申し込む

in bad shape ひどい状態で

22

Narrator: Proposals tend to happen at night, around the time that the tower's lights become visible to the entire city. Twenty thousand bulbs have covered ³⁰ the structure since the year 2000, and on top a ray of light appears to circle the summit. And the lamps are currently under repair — an operation overseen by electronics manager Jacques Barrière. With so much technology 320 metres up, it isn't ³⁵ a job for the ⁵(   ) of heart. But Barrière says he's always loved the top of the tower — even getting the chance to stand atop the ⁶(   ).

bulb 電球
ray of light 一筋の光
oversee 監督する
electronics manager 主任
電気技師

atop... 〜の頂上に

Jacques Barrière: When you really go to the top — to the top of ⁴⁰ the antenna — it's fabulous. It's fabulous because you're in the sky. You're in the sky, and you see all of Paris.

fabulous 信じられない

Narrator: It's a view not many will get to experience, but the city of Paris can enjoy the ⁷(   ) ⁴⁵ from a distance. Repairs to the lamps are scheduled to wind up in two weeks, after which time the Iron Lady will shine once more.

be scheduled to... 〜する予
定である
wind up 終了する

● *COMPREHENSION*

1 については質問に対する答えを、2 については下線部に入るものを選びましょう。

1. What do we learn about the Eiffel Tower's elevators?
   (A) They all use state-of-the-art modern technology.
   (B) People rarely make marriage proposals inside them.
   (C) The first ones of the day carry no passengers.
   (D) They are currently under repair.

2. Marriage proposals on the Eiffel Tower _____ to happen in the evening.
   (A) used   (B) seem   (C) expect   (D) tend

PRESENTING THE CONTENTS

次の英文は、スクリプトの要点をプレゼンテーションのスピーチ形式にまとめたものです。音声を聴いて、空所に入る語句を記入しましょう。

The Eiffel Tower has been an iconic tourist attraction for more than 120 years. Let's take a look at some of its features. The first elevators of the day go up empty so that they can be tested. The elevator cables are regularly checked with 1)_____ and completely changed every seven years, just like the exterior paint. The tower is a popular spot for people to 2)_____ marriage. These proposals tend to happen at night, around the time when the tower's lights become visible to the entire city. Since the year 2000, the structure has been covered with 20,000 bulbs, and on top, a ray of light appears to circle the 3)_____. The lamps are currently being 4)_____, but once these repairs to the lamps are completed, "the Iron Lady" will shine once more.

PINPOINT

英語では、先行する情報に後続して説明を追加する「後置修飾」が多用されます。主な「後置修飾」の手段は、次のとおりです。

・関係詞（節）—関係代名詞や関係副詞	・不定詞（句）	・形容詞（句）
・分詞（句）—現在分詞や過去分詞	・前置詞（句）	

英文の空所に入る適切な語を枠内から選びましょう。

1. The Eiffel Tower is a high-rise tourist attraction _____ the city of Paris.

2. Gustave Eiffel was a civil engineer _____ designed many distinctive iron constructions.

3. A ride in one of the tower's elevators is a chance _____ fly over the city.

4. Wilhelm Dubelloy is a tower guide _____ many years of experience.

5. The viewing deck of the tower is a very romantic place _____ to pop the question.

with	suitable	who	overlooking	to

● *FURTHER INVESTIGATION*

建築図面は、建築家が自身のアイデアを発展させたり、あるいは建築家・施工業者・依頼主の間のコミュニケーションを深化させたりするための、重要なツールです。

A 次の図面の名称に対応する英語を選びましょう。

1. 正面図	(　)	a. floor plan	
2. 断面図	(　)	b. cross section	
3. 平面図	(　)	c. perspective	
4. パース	(　)	d. front elevation	

B 次の図面に該当する名称を、A の a~d から選びましょう。。

1. (　　　　　　)

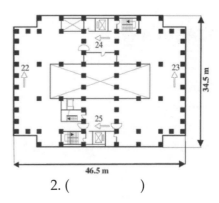

2. (　　　　　　)

3. (　　　　　　)

4. (　　　　　　)

Drone for the Disabled

UNIT 6

没入型包摂のワクワク感

誰もが共生できる社会的包摂（social inclusion）の実現に、現代の科学技術は大きな役割を果たします。たとえば、活動的な日常を突然の事故で失った人も、没入型（immersive）ヴァーチャルリアリティなどの先端技術を活用して、これまで同等の、あるいはそれ以上の "リアル" な興奮を得ることが可能です。

VOCABULARY

CD 1-23

A 次の語句に対応する日本語を選びましょう。

1.	paralysed	（　　）	a.	電動車椅子サッカー
2.	immerse	（　　）	b.	生み出す
3.	power soccer	（　　）	c.	オートバイ
4.	motorbike/motorcycle	（　　）	d.	没入させる
5.	generate	（　　）	e.	麻痺した

B 次の語句の下線部と同じ発音が含まれる語を、A の語句から１つずつ選びましょう。

1.　ATV <u>a</u>ccident「ATV（= all-terrain vehicle [全地形万能車]）での事故」　　　　（　　　）

2.　racing dr<u>o</u>ne「レース用ドローン」　　　　（　　　）

3.　v<u>ir</u>tual reality headset「ヴァーチャルリアリティ用ヘッドセット」　　　（　　　）

FINDING THE TOPIC

WEB動画 / DVD

次の英文が映像の内容と合っている場合は T を、合っていない場合は F を選びましょう。

1. Agustin Zanoli was left paralysed as a result of a motorbike accident.　　T / F

2. Agustin's accident prevented him from studying at university.　　T / F

3. Daniel Sequeiros was at first reluctant to allow Agustin to try to pilot the drone.　　T / F

CHECKING THE SCRIPT

WEB動画 🖥 DVD 💿 CD 💿 1-24

Ⓐ 音声を聴いて、空所に入る語を書き取りましょう。
Ⓑ スクリプトを読んで、内容を把握しましょう。

Agustin Zanoli: quadriplegic drone pilot
Daniel Sequeiros: aeronautical engineer

Narrator: Growing up, Agustin Zanoli was always on the hunt for adrenaline. He rode motorbikes and ATVs, and enjoyed skiing in his native Argentina. But in 2012, just a few weeks shy of his high school graduation, an ATV accident left him ¹(   ) 5 from the neck down.

Agustin Zanoli: Right when I had the accident, I realised something bad had happened, because at that moment I couldn't move any more. But I never thought it was going to be so serious. 10

Narrator: Despite his dramatic injuries, Agustin stayed on track with most of his plans. He began studying mechanical engineering at university, and took up ²(   ) soccer. But the adrenaline rush was missing — that is, until a friend heard 15 aeronautical engineer Daniel Sequeiros speaking about racing ³(   ) at a conference, and contacted him to see if it would be possible for Agustin to get involved in the sport.

Daniel Sequeiros: At first, I said, "No, he won't be able to fly", 20 because you need to be able to hold the remote control. But I started to think, and I said, "No, something can be developed so that Agustin can fly".

Narrator: Using a ⁴(   ) reality headset that 25 interprets head movements, Agustin can fly the drone hands-free. A mouthpiece lets him dictate the speed, which can reach up to 100 kilometres

on the hunt for ... 〜を追い求める

adrenaline （= adrenaline rush）アドレナリンによる興奮
A shy of B BまでにAが足りない
from the neck down 首から下が
stay on track 順調に物事をすすめる

take up 始める

aeronautical engineer 航空技師
conference 会議
get involved in... 〜に参加する

interpret 解釈する
hands-free 手を使わずに
dictate 決定する
reach up to... 〜まで到達する

27

per hour. The drone's camera lets him choose his course and ⁵(　　　　　　　　) himself in the flight, evoking that rush he loves.

Agustín Zanoli: Flying a racing drone gives me back that same adrenaline that the ATV or motorcycle gave me. And the adrenaline it ⁶(　　　　　　) is wonderful.

evoke 呼び起こす

Narrator: For his part, Sequeiros has never thought about charging for his invention, and hopes it can bring joy to others.

for one's part ～としては

charge for... ～の代金を請求する

Daniel Sequeiros: I want it to be reproducible everywhere for people in the same condition as Agustin, so they can feel the adrenaline you feel when you're flying and going really fast without any risk.

reproducible 再現できる

Narrator: An accident may have stopped Agustin from riding ⁷(　　　　　　　), but with a bit of technology, he now has the opportunity to fly.

● COMPREHENSION

1 については質問に対する答えを、2 については下線部に入るものを選びましょう。

1. What is NOT true of Agustin?
    (A) The only part of his body that he can move is his head.
    (B) He can fly the drone without using his hands.
    (C) Playing power soccer gave him a feeling of great excitement.
    (D) He does not have to pay the engineer to use his device.

2. _____ his serious injuries, Agustin was able to study at university.
    (A) In spite
    (B) Despite
    (C) Even
    (D) However

PRESENTING THE CONTENTS 🎵 CD 1-25

次の英文は、スクリプトの要点をプレゼンテーションのスピーチ形式にまとめたものです。
音声を聴いて、空所に入る語句を記入しましょう。

Technology can help disabled people realise their dreams. Agustin Zanoli, from Argentina, loved riding motorbikes and ATVs, and also enjoyed skiing. But in 2012, shortly before his high school graduation, an ATV accident left him 1)_____ from the neck down. Despite his disability, Agustin began studying mechanical engineering at university and took up power soccer. But he missed the 2)_____ rush that his former hobbies had given him. A friend wondered whether racing drones might be suitable for Agustin. He approached Daniel Sequeiros, an 3)_____ engineer, to see if Agustin could get involved in the sport. After first refusing, Sequeiros reconsidered and built a device that allows Agustin to control the drone 4)_____ through head movements. Sequeiros has never thought about charging for his invention and hopes it can bring others joy.

PINPOINT

情報を効率的に付け加える方法の一つとして、現在分詞／過去分詞に導かれる分詞構文の利用が有効です。生起する位置は、文頭・文中・文尾のいずれの場合もありえます。

（例）[文頭] Using a virtual reality headset, Agustin can fly the drone hands-free.
[文中] Agustin, using a virtual reality headset, can fly the drone hands-free.
[文尾] Agustin can fly the drone hands-free, using a virtual reality headset.
「ヴァーチャルリアリティ用ヘッドセットを使って、アグスティンは手を使わずにドローンを操縦することができます。」

次の英文の（　）内の動詞を適切な形に変えましょう。

1. Agustin had an accident when driving an ATV, (leave → _____) him paralysed from the neck down.

2. (move → _____) by Agustin's determination to join the drone race, Sequeiros worked on a volunteer basis.

3. Sequeiros does not intend to patent his device, (hope → _____) that the technology will be duplicated elsewhere in the world.

FURTHER INVESTIGATION

工学（engineering）の諸分野は、人類の多様な営みを映し出す"鏡"として、時代の変遷とともに細分化・融合を重ねています。

A 次の工学分野について、対応する日本語名称を選びましょう。

1. Aeronautical / Aerospace engineering	（　）	a. 電気工学
2. Biomedical engineering	（　）	b. 環境工学
3. Civil engineering	（　）	c. 農業工学
4. Architectural engineering	（　）	d. 化学工学
5. Electrical engineering	（　）	e. 土木工学
6. Control engineering	（　）	f. 生体医工学
7. Chemical engineering	（　）	g. 材料工学／材料科学
8. Environmental engineering	（　）	h. 制御工学
9. Materials science and engineering	（　）	i. 建築工学
10. Agricultural engineering	（　）	j. 航空工学

B 次の英文の空所に入る適切な工学分野を、A の 1 〜 10 から選びましょう。

1. ＿＿＿＿ is an interdisciplinary field concerning the properties of matter and its applications to various areas of science and engineering.

2. ＿＿＿＿ applies science and technology to production and processing in the field of agriculture, and to the management of harvests.

3. ＿＿＿＿ is a discipline that explores knowledge in engineering, biology and medicine to improve human health.

Crucial Minutes

アメリカ版緊急地震速報

太平洋沿岸は、巨大地震の多発地帯。日本だけでなく、海の向こうの米国も、大きな被害を未然に防ぐべく、わずかな地震波をつぶさに解析する警報システムの構築に必死です。「シェイク・アラート（ShakeAlert）」は、その最先端の開発成果。システムの精度を高めつつ、一刻も早い実用化が期待されています。

VOCABULARY

1-27

A 次の語句に対応する日本語を選びましょう。

1. duck   (   )   a. 地震計
2. prediction   (   )   b. 警戒
3. wave   (   )   c. 予測
4. seismometer   (   )   d. かがむ
5. precaution   (   )   e. 地震波

B 次の語句の下線部と同じ発音が含まれる語を、A の語句から 1 つずつ選びましょう。

1. early warning system「早期警報システム」   (   )

2. 'drop, cover and hold'「かがむ、身を隠す、そしてつかまる」   (   )

3. ShakeAlert「シェイク・アラート」
   （米国地質調査所を中核として開発されている地震早期警報システム）   (   )

FINDING THE TOPIC

次の英文が映像の内容と合っている場合は T を、合っていない場合は F を選びましょう。

1. In the event of an earthquake, the system will automatically stop
   high-speed trains and high-rise elevators.   T / F

2. The earthquake detection devices are located both on land and at sea.   T / F

3. The early warning system is not yet ready for the public to use.   T / F

CHECKING THE SCRIPT

A 音声を聴いて、空所に入る語を書き取りましょう。
B スクリプトを読んで、内容を把握しましょう。

Barb Graff: Director of Emergency Management, City of Seattle

John Vidale: Director, Pacific Northwest Seismic Network

Alert system: Earthquake. Duck, cover and…

Narrator: Alerts sent directly to cellphones, companies and government agencies — warning of a seismic event. Agencies, like Seattle's emergency coordinating center, are testing an early ¹(   ) 5 system for a possible major earthquake off the coast of the Pacific Northwest of the United States.

government agency 行政機関
emergency coordinating center 緊急事態調整センター
coast of the Pacific Northwest 太平洋岸北西部

Barb Graff: What it'll enable us to do is to let people take a protective action like 'drop, cover and ²(   ).' They can stop things 10 like high-speed trains or high-rise elevators and surgeries, and take a protective action. It will let us save more lives and protect more property.

protective action 身を守る行動
high-rise 高層の
property 財産
moderate 中規模の

Narrator: For most moderate earthquakes, the warning could be as little as 15 to 30 seconds. But it's 15 ³(   ) that the west coast is overdue a so-called 'big one,' a potential 9-plus magnitude earthquake that would cause widespread devastation and destruction, that is driving the installation of an alert system that 20 could give as much as a five-minute life-saving warning. At the heart of the system are hundreds of ⁴(   ) spread across the Pacific Northwest and offshore.

be overdue... 〜が起きてもおかしくない

devastation 荒廃

drive 駆り立てる
installation 設置

offshore 沖で
estimate 推定する

John Vidale: The ⁵(   ) system works by 25 our many seismometers noticing the earthquake. The closest instruments see it first. We quickly estimate the size of the earthquake from the fastest ⁶(   ), and then calculate what

shaking should result from this earthquake, and
send the wording out to the people who need to
take [7](   ).

30

wording 通知

Narrator: More than 1,000 minor earthquakes are recorded in
Washington State every year. The vast majority are
not strong enough to cause any noticeable ground
movement.

35

vast majority 圧倒的多数

John Vidale: Sorry.

Alert system: Earthquake. No shaking expected in three
seconds.

John Vidale: Three point three… Huh, we could have felt that.
That was the early warning system, by the way.

40

Narrator: The early warning system is still at least a year
away from being available to the public. It's a race
against time, as a catastrophic 9-plus magnitude
earthquake hits the Pacific Northwest, on average,
once every 240 years. The last one was more than
300 years ago, and many fear the next 'big one' is
already well overdue.

45

catastrophic 壊滅的な

on average 平均で

COMPREHENSION

1 については質問に対する答えを、2 については下線部に入るものを選びましょう。

1. What is the main purpose of the new system?
   (A) To predict when the next giant earthquake will occur
   (B) To alert people when a noticeable quake is imminent
   (C) To count the number of earthquakes that occur each year
   (D) To increase the number of seismometers in the Pacific Northwest

2. If people know about an earthquake in advance, they can take necessary _____.
   (A) predictions   (B) preparations   (C) precautions   (D) prescriptions

次の英文は、スクリプトの要点をプレゼンテーションのスピーチ形式にまとめたものです。
音声を聴いて、空所に入る語句を記入しましょう。

It is impossible to escape an earthquake. The most effective countermeasure is a system that can 1)_____ earthquakes in advance and allow people to take necessary precautions. I will look at a system being tested in the Pacific Northwest region of the U.S. Seismometers located on land and at sea throughout the region pick up shaking and relay a message to the control center, where experts calculate the size of the quake and 2)_____ the shaking it will cause. If they judge that the quake is serious enough, they will issue an 3)_____ to people's cellphones, companies and government agencies. Even with short notice, people will still be able to protect themselves. This will be especially valuable in the event of a 9-plus 4)_____ earthquake, which hits the region on average once every 240 years.

● **PINPOINT**

副詞や形容詞が "as…as" の間にはさまれた場合、その度合い・数量が強調されることがあります。

> （例）For most moderate earthquakes, the warning could be as little as 15 to 30 seconds.
> 「たいていの中規模地震に対して、警報はわずか15〜30秒程度の長さになるでしょう。」

日本語を参考にして、英語の空所に入る適切な語を枠内から選びましょう。

1. as _____ as a 9-plus magnitude earthquake
   「マグニチュード9以上の地震ほどもある大きさの」

2. as _____ as a five-minute life-saving warning
   「5分ほどもたっぷり継続する人命救助警報」

3. as _____ as in the last 10 years of the 20th century
   「20世紀の最後の10年にはすでに」

much	large	early

FURTHER INVESTIGATION

次の表は、世界における巨大地震を一覧にしたものです。下記の英文の内容が正しいものにはTを、誤っているものにはFを記入しましょう。

13 Largest Earthquakes in the World

	Mag	Location	Name	Date
1	9.5	Bio-Bio, Chile	Valdivia Earthquake	1960-05-22
2	9.2	Southern Alaska	1964 Great Alaska Earthquake	1964-03-28
3	9.1	Off the West Coast of Northern Sumatra	2004 Sumatra Earthquake	2004-12-26
3	9.1	Near the East Coast of Honshu, Japan	West Japan Earthquake	2011-03-11
5	9.0	Off the East Coast of the Kamchatka Peninsula, Russia	Kamchatka Earthquake	1952-11-04
6	8.8	Offshore Bio-Bio, Chile	Maule Earthquake	2010-02-27
6	8.8	Near the Coast of Ecuador	1906 Ecuador–Colombia Earthquake	1906-01-31
8	8.7	Rat Islands, Aleutian Islands, Alaska	Rat Islands Earthquake	1965-02-04
9	8.6	Eastern Xizang-India border region	Assam, Tibet Earthquake	1950-08-15
9	8.6	Off the West Coast of Northern Sumatra	2012 Sumatra Earthquake	2012-04-11
9	8.6	Northern Sumatra, Indonesia	Nias Earthquake	2005-03-28
9	8.6	Andreanof Islands, Aleutian Islands, Alaska	1957 Alaska Earthquake	1957-03-09
9	8.6	South of Alaska	Unimak Island Earthquake	1946-04-01

(Based on the data from the U.S. Geological Survey)

1. (   ) The largest earthquake in the world in history occurred in Chili in Latin America.

2. (   ) Most of the earthquakes on the list occurred along the coast of the Atlantic Ocean.

3. (   ) Judging from the list, Sumatra is the place with the greatest concentration of large earthquakes in history.

4. (   ) Nearly half of the listed earthquakes occurred intensively in 1950s and 1960s.

Mites vs Parasites

UNIT 8

"虫には虫"の有機農業

世界的な健康食ブームの中で、化学肥料や殺虫剤を抑えて栽培した野菜に消費者の注目が集まっています。その需要に応えるべく、有害な寄生虫を別の虫に食べさせて駆除する農法が考案されました。一見、環境に優しい農法に見えますが、逆にその地域の生物多様性に悪影響をもたらす危険も指摘されています。

VOCABULARY

🎧 CD 1-31

A 次の語句に対応する日本語を選びましょう。

1. biofactory （　　）
2. resist （　　）
3. certify （　　）
4. symbiosis （　　）
5. greenhouse （　　）

a. 共生関係
b. 温室
c. 耐える
d. バイオ工場
e. 認可する

B 次の語句の下線部と同じ発音が含まれる語を、A の語句から 1 つずつ選びましょう。

1. large-scale industrial <u>a</u>griculture 「大規模工業型農業」 （　　）

2. pesticide-f<u>ree</u> pest control 「殺虫剤を使わない害虫抑制法」 （　　）

3. biodi<u>ver</u>sity 「生物多様性」 （　　）

FINDING THE TOPIC

WEB動画 💻 / DVD 💿

次の英文が映像の内容と合っている場合は T を、合っていない場合は F を選びましょう。

1. Antonio uses pesticides to kill the parasites that threaten his crops. T / F

2. The expression "plastic sea" refers to the large amount of garbage that can be found floating in the Mediterranean. T / F

3. More and more farmers are avoiding the use of pesticides because of public opinion. T / F

CHECKING THE SCRIPT

WEB動画 DVD CD 1-32

Ａ 音声を聴いて、空所に入る語を書き取りましょう。
Ｂ スクリプトを読んで、内容を把握しましょう。

Antonio Zamora: pepper farmer

Maria José Pardo: Director-General of Bioline of the InVivo group

Koldo Hernandez: member of the "Ecologists in Action" association

Narrator: Every morning, Antonio checks that his peppers have survived the night and haven't been attacked by parasites. Pesticides were the tried and tested method for fighting pests, but since 2007, Antonio has been using natural pest control — small bags of 5 insects that eat the parasites that threaten his crop.

parasite 寄生虫
crop 収穫物

Antonio Zamora: Insects are constantly working. You let them go one day and they work all day, all week, all month. How does it work? Well, there is a kind of ¹(   ) between the plant and 10 insects, which means that the plant produces more and more, and gets healthier, as does its immediate environment.

immediate 周囲の

Narrator: Antonio's pesticide-free peppers are found in the middle of a "plastic sea" — 30,000 hectares 15 of ²(   ) bordering the Mediterranean, a notorious symbol of large-scale industrial agriculture. Two-point-five million tonnes of tomatoes, cucumbers, courgettes, peppers, and aubergines grow here year-round. 20 Since 2007, insecticide use has decreased by 40% in the province of Almeria. Faced with growing insecticide ³(   ) and mounting consumer pressure, farmers in the region are increasingly avoiding chemicals. French 25 agricultural giant InVivo has invested 15 million euros to create a ⁴(   ) in the heart

"plastic sea"「プラスチックの海」（プラスチック製温室の集合体）
border 接する
the Mediterranean 地中海
notorious 悪名高い
courgette ズッキーニ

aubergine ナス

insecticide 殺虫剤

province of Almeria アルメリア県（スペイン南部の県）

mount 増大する

agricultural giant InVivo 巨大農業企業インビーボー社

of the "plastic sea", raising billions of mites to be released against parasites.

raise 育てる

María José Pardo: The objective is to produce 100,000 billion insects to be able to supply these markets, and achieve a turnover of more than 10 million euros in one year. 30

objective 目的

turnover 売上高

Narrator: For environmental associations, pesticide-[5](   ) pest control is a positive step forward, though some concerns remain to be addressed. 35

environmental association 環境保護団体

address 取り組む

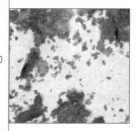

Koldo Hernandez: It is an agricultural practice that, even if it is more ecological, does not respect the natural rhythms of production, the natural rhythms of fields, the natural rhythms of agriculture. It does not respect the [6](   ) of the soil, and still requires a series of certified agrochemical products, pesticides and fertilisers. 40

soil 土壌
agrochemical product 農薬
fertiliser 肥料

Narrator: Ecologists recommend organic farming practices as they reduce pesticide use. But, with only 2,000 hectares of [7](   ) crops, organic farming represents less than 7% of the crops in the "plastic sea". 45

represent 相当する

COMPREHENSION

1 については質問に対する答えを、2 については下線部に入るものを選びましょう。

1. What is the company InVivo doing?
    (A) Certifying vegetables
    (B) Raising insects
    (C) Developing pesticides
    (D) Building organic farms

2. The new pest control method relies on a symbiosis _____ plants and insects.
    (A) toward   (B) against   (C) among   (D) between

● *PRESENTING THE CONTENTS*

 1-33

次の英文は、スクリプトの要点をプレゼンテーションのスピーチ形式にまとめたものです。
音声を聴いて、空所に入る語句を記入しましょう。

To protect his vegetables from pests, Antonio does not use pesticide. Instead, he uses insects that eat the parasites that 1)_____ his crops. He says there is a kind of 2)_____ between the plant and insects, and so the plant produces more, and gets healthier, as does its immediate environment. Antonio grows vegetables in a so-called "plastic sea", a large area of greenhouses bordering the Mediterranean Sea in Spain. Farmers there are 3)_____ avoiding chemicals because of growing insecticide resistance and consumer pressure. The implications of this approach need to be examined in greater detail. Some people are against it because it does not respect the rhythms of nature or the 4)_____ of the soil, and still requires chemicals and fertilisers.

● *PINPOINT*

「目的・目標」を簡潔に表す表現の一つに、"主語＋ be 動詞＋ to 不定詞" があります。

（例) The objective is to produce 100,000 billion insects to be able to supply the markets.
「目的は、市場に供給することができるように100兆匹の昆虫を生産することです。」

[　] 内の語句を適切な語順に並べかえ、英文を完成させましょう。

1. One of the three missions of InVivo _____
   _____ food solutions.

   [to / new sustainable / bring about / is]

2. Antonio's intention _____ are
   as healthy as possible.

   [produce vegetables / is / that / just to]

3. The supreme goal of modern agriculture _____
   _____ as well as eco-friendliness.

   [to / the natural rhythms of agriculture / is / respect]

●*FURTHER INVESTIGATION*

円グラフ (pie chart) は、各項目が全体の中で占める割合を示す際に有効なチャートです。

次の円グラフは、農林水産省が「有機農業」「オーガニック」という語の認知度について調査した結果を示すものです。下記の英文の空所に入る数値と、必要な場合は単位を記入しましょう。

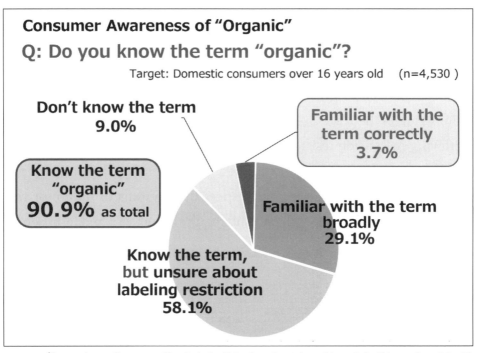

Consumer Awareness of "Organic"

Q: Do you know the term "organic"?

Target: Domestic consumers over 16 years old   (n=4,530)

Don't know the term
9.0%

Familiar with the term correctly
3.7%

Know the term "organic"
90.9% as total

Familiar with the term broadly
29.1%

Know the term, but unsure about labeling restriction
58.1%

(Source: https://www.maff.go.jp/e/policies/env/sustainagri/attach/pdf/organicagri-1.pdf)

1. The total number of respondents who answered the question is _____.

2. The percentage of people who are somewhat familiar with the term is nearly _____.

3. The biggest group consists of consumers who know the term but are not sure about the restriction on labeling, with a rate of _____.

4. The number of consumers who know something about the term is _____ times more than the number of people who do not know it.

Gearing up for a New Top Speed

地上最速への疾走

有人自動車で音速を超える―この挑戦に成功したのは歴史上 1 台だけ、人類史上 1 人だけです。1997年に達成したこの偉業の記録保持者アンディ・グリーンは、新たなロケット自動車ブラッドハウンド LSR を駆り、南アフリカの乾燥しきった砂漠の真ん中で、人類が開発する工学の限界に再度挑戦しています。

VOCABULARY

🎵 1-35

A 次の語句に対応する日本語を選びましょう。

1. phase   (　　)
2. inspire   (　　)
3. achieve   (　　)
4. stretch   (　　)
5. power   (　　)

a. 広い土地
b. 動機を与える
c. 動力源になる
d. 段階
e. 達成する

B 次の語句の下線部と同じ発音が含まれる語を、A の語句から 1 つずつ選びましょう。

1. four lightweight aluminium wh<u>ee</u>ls 「軽量アルミニウムの 4 輪」　　(　　)

2. br<u>a</u>ke horsepower 「ブレーキ馬力」　　(　　)

3. high-performance j<u>e</u>t fighter 「高性能のジェット戦闘機」　　(　　)

FINDING THE TOPIC

WEB動画 🖥️　DVD 💿

次の英文が映像の内容と合っている場合は T を、合っていない場合は F を選びましょう。

1. Bloodhound has not yet completed its final model of the high-speed car.　　T / F

2. The test-runs of the car are being conducted next to a lake in the Kalahari Desert.　　T / F

3. Andy Green believes there are similarities between flying a fighter jet and driving the Bloodhound car.　　T / F

● CHECKING THE SCRIPT

WEB動画　DVD　CD　1-36

A 音声を聴いて、空所に入る語を書き取りましょう。
B スクリプトを読んで、内容を把握しましょう。

Andy Green: Bloodhound LSR driver

Mark Chapman: head engineer at Bloodhound

Ian Warhurst: owner, Bloodhound LSR

Narrator: Rocketing up to 900 kilometres an hour, in South
Africa's Kalahari Desert, this car, created by British
company Bloodhound, is still in its testing phase.
They hope to get to the point where it can compete
to break the land speed record of 1,223 kilometres　5
an hour, the fastest speed ¹(　　　　　　　　)
by a person in a vehicle on land.

Andy Green: That's 900 kilometres now out of the way. We're
now gonna target something round about 980 and
see how that goes. And if we can get that fast, we'll　10
see if we can sneak it up towards 1,000. That is
about as fast as we can go on the 16 kilometres we
have available here.

Narrator: The 16-kilometre ²(　　　　　　　　) is located
in the bed of a dried-out lake in the Kalahari Desert,　15
one of few places in the world flat enough to shoot for
such speeds. The vehicle is ³(　　　　　　　　)
by a fighter plane's jet engine, which will later be
reinforced with an additional one from a rocket.
And it's all carried on top of four lightweight　20
aluminium wheels.

Mark Chapman: The total power while we're in South
Africa this year is about 50,000…54,000 brake
⁴(　　　　　　　　), which is like 9 tons of
thrust.　25

Narrator: When it comes to finding a qualified driver, you'd
struggle to do better than Andy Green, holder of

Kalahari Desert カラハ
リ砂漠
Bloodhound ブラッドハ
ウンド社（陸上走行の最
速記録更新をねらうベン
チャー）
compete 立ち向かう

out of the way 驚くべき

sneak it up もう少し進む

dried-out 干上がった
shoot for... 〜に向かって
取り組む
reinforce 強化する

thrust 推進力

qualified 適任の
struggle 悪戦苦闘する

42

the current land speed record since 1997 and a
fighter pilot in Britain's Royal Air Force.

Andy Green: The skill sets needed in terms of monitoring the ₃₀
high speed, controlling it, making the decisions
based on a considered response of the "Does
this look right? Is it safe to carry on?" — that is
exactly like flying a, you know, high-performance
jet ⁵(   ) at the limits of its ₃₅
performance.

Narrator: But this major operation — setting up the vehicles,
staff and infrastructure in the middle of a desert
— comes with an inevitable carbon footprint.
Bloodhound recognise this but hope that their ₄₀
activities will have a net positive impact in the long
run.

Ian Warhurst: This project ⁶(   ) people to do
engineering, and we're going to solve the problems
in the future with more engineers developing ₄₅
new technologies, becoming faster, more efficient,
becoming carbon neutral.

Narrator: With the first ⁷(   ) of testing
complete, Bloodhound are back in the UK, with
their return to the South African desert planned for ₅₀
the summer of 2021. By then, they hope to come
equipped with an extra rocket engine — the boost
that, they hope, will enable them to set a new land
speed record.

Britain's Royal Air Force
英国王立空軍

considered response
熟考した反応

carbon footprint 二酸化炭
素の排出

net 完全な
in the long run 長期的には

carbon neutral カーボンニュ
ートラルな（二酸化炭素の排
出と吸収のバランスが取れて
いる状態）

boost 推力強化

● *COMPREHENSION*

1 については質問に対する答えを、2 については下線部に入るものを選びましょう。

1. What speed has the Bloodhound high-speed car achieved so far?
   (A) 900 kph (B) 980 kph (C) 1,000 kph (D) 1,223 kph

2. The vehicle _____ by a jet engine from a fighter plane.
   (A) powers (B) powered (C) is powered (D) is powering

次の英文は、スクリプトの要点をプレゼンテーションのスピーチ形式にまとめたものです。
音声を聴いて、空所に入る語句を記入しましょう。

British company Bloodhound is testing a car that it hopes will break the world land speed record of 1,223 kph. Testing is happening on a 16-kilometre 1)_____ in a dried-out lake in the Kalahari Desert in South Africa, one of few places in the world 2)_____ enough to make such speeds possible. The important point to note is that the vehicle is powered by a jet engine from a fighter plane and will later get an 3)_____ one from a rocket. Its driver has held the current land speed record since 1997 and is a pilot in the British air force. Setting up vehicles, staff, and infrastructure in the middle of a desert creates a heavy carbon 4)_____, but the company hopes to reduce this.

● *PINPOINT*

"主語＋動詞＋目的語＋ to 不定詞" という構文で使用される動詞は、expect / force / want / request / warn など多数あります。いずれも "目的語＋ to 不定詞" の部分がこの文で 2 つ目の「主部＋述部」の関係を構成します。

（例） This project inspires people to do engineering.
　　　主部①＋述部①　　　　主部②＋述部②
「このプロジェクトは、人々に工学に取り組む動機を与えます。」

[ ] 内の語句を適切な語順に並べかえ、英文を完成させましょう。

1. Bloodhound _____the land speed record again.

   [challenge / to / asked / Andy Green]

2. The new vehicle _____ a speed of over 900 kilometres per hour.

   [to already / enabled / Green / reach]

3. The IPCC _____ CO_2 emissions.

   [the global community / to / requires / significantly reduce]

FURTHER INVESTIGATION

定義文（definition sentence）は、項目・概念などを明確に定める構文で、情報の発信者と受信者の間でコミュニケーションの効率を確保します。

◆ 定義文の構造

Bloodhound is a British venture that pursues a new land speed record.

項目・概念など	述語	カテゴリー	前後を結びつける文法要素	特徴的な内容

                （e.g.）be動詞   （e.g.）関係代名詞

                        refer to   分詞

                        be defined as   前置詞

「カテゴリー」と「前後を結びつける文法要素」を選択肢から選び、次の1～5の定義文を完成させましょう。

1. Andy Green is _____ _____ has been World Land Speed Record holder for over two decades.

2. Bloodhound LSR is classified as _____ _____ with a fighter plane's jet engine.

3. Supersonic speed refers to _____ _____ faster than the speed of sound.

4. The Kalahari Desert is _____ _____ the south of the African continent.

5. The land speed record is _____ _____ by a manned vehicle on land.

カテゴリー	前後を結びつける文法要素
the speed of an object	travelling
one of the world's largest deserts	achieved
the highest speed	in
a land vehicle	who
a fighter pilot	equipped

New Skin from a Printer

人工皮膚移植の進化形

3D (three-dimensional) プリンターは、その登場以来、ものづくりの仕組みを大きく変えました。建築や機械、装飾品や宇宙開発など、プリントする材料を変えることで応用範囲はますます拡大しています。なかでも注目されるのが医療の分野。特に 3D バイオプリンティング（bioprinting）は、急速に重要性を増しています。

VOCABULARY   CD 1-39

A 次の語句に対応する日本語を選びましょう。

1. tissue   (　　)   a. 臓器
2. epidermis   (　　)   b. 移植
3. organ   (　　)   c. 組織
4. transplant   (　　)   d. コラーゲン
5. collagen   (　　)   e. 表皮

B 次の語句の下線部と同じ発音が含まれる語を、A の語句から 1 つずつ選びましょう。

1. inkjet technology「インクジェット技術」
   （液状のインク粒子を飛ばして対象物に非接触で印刷する技術）   (　　)

2. predefined computer model「事前に規定されたコンピュータモデル」   (　　)

3. French (National) Institute of Health and Medical Research
   「フランス国立保健医学研究機構」   (　　)

FINDING THE TOPIC   WEB動画 / DVD

次の英文が映像の内容と合っている場合は T を、合っていない場合は F を選びましょう。

1. Human cells are mixed with ink to form collagen.   T / F

2. At first, the new cells are almost impossible to see without using a
   microscope.   T / F

3. Skin cells created in this way could be valuable for companies that
   need to test cosmetics or drugs.   T / F

CHECKING THE SCRIPT

WEB動画 ☐🎬 DVD 💿 CD 1-40

A 音声を聴いて、空所に入る語を書き取りましょう。
B スクリプトを読んで、内容を把握しましょう。

Fabien Guillemot: founder of biotech firm Poietis, ex-researcher at French Institute of Health and Medical Research

Marine Salducci: biological engineer

Narrator: It's a technology like no other. The scientists entering this lab near Bordeaux have created bio-printers capable of printing three-dimensional human tissue, a global first according to its creators. The first step is gathering human cells to farm them. 5
The cells are found in hospitals and are mixed with ¹( ) to form the 'ink'.

Fabien Guillemot: Bio-printing with lasers works a bit like ²( ) technology, in the sense that a laser drive creates a spurt of ink, the ink 10 being a sort of cradle for cells. By moving the laser beam, we lay drops of cells at different locations and rebuild 3D structures layer by layer.

Narrator: The result is practically invisible to the naked eye. But, under a microscope, it's a different 15 story. The cells are alive. And, by following a ³( ) computer model, they start interacting with each other. After a few days, a brand-new ⁴( ) begins to take shape. 20

Marine Salducci: The tissue comes to life after printing. Normally, when printed, the tissue is the size of the small circle, so it actually contracts under the influence of the cells.

Narrator: The company and its 20-odd employees are 25 currently using printers created with the help of the French Institute of Health and Medical ⁵( ), which is also working

lab (=laboratory) 研究室

Bordeaux ボルドー (仏南西部の都市)
bio-printer バイオプリンター

farm 培養する

laser drive レーザー照射装置
spurt 噴出
cradle ゆりかご
layer by layer 一層ずつ
practically 実際には
microscope 顕微鏡

brand-new 真新しい

come to life 生命を宿す

contract 収縮する
20-odd 20人余りの
work towards... ～に向けて取り組む

47

towards making its own printer.

Fabien Guillemot: With laser technology, we have a resolution ₃₀ of around 20 micrometres. So we can print cells cell by cell, and give even more complexity to what we create, and reproduce all the complexity we see in our tissue and our ⁶(   ).

Narrator: The technology has already generated interest. ₃₅ Cosmetic and pharmaceutical laboratories could use the 'skin' to test new substances and assess their toxicity. Good news for industries in which cosmetic testing on animals has been outlawed since 2013. But Poietis is aiming for more than that. ₄₀ In 10 years, it's hoping its printers can print skin from the cells of medical patients, to use that skin for grafts and ⁷(   ) and one day — who knows — to even print skin directly onto patients. ₄₅

resolution 分解能（細かく
細分・識別する能力）

generate interest 興味を
引き起こす
pharmaceutical 製薬の
toxicity 毒性
outlaw 法的に禁止する

Poietis ポイエティス社（仏
のバイオテクノロジー企業）

graft 移植

COMPREHENSION

1 については質問に対する答えを、2 については下線部に入るものを選びましょう。

1. In what way does the French Institute of Health and Medical Research help the company?

   (A) It provides the company with the human skin cells that it needs.

   (B) It played a part in making the printers that the company uses.

   (C) It designed and built the computers that the company uses.

   (D) It provides the company with research material.

2. The bio-printers are _____ of printing three-dimensional human tissue.

   (A) capable

   (B) able

   (C) prepared

   (D) designed

PRESENTING THE CONTENTS

 1-41

次の英文は、スクリプトの要点をプレゼンテーションのスピーチ形式にまとめたものです。
音声を聴いて、空所に入る語句を記入しましょう。

> I'm sure everyone has a basic familiarity with idea of 3D printing, which can be used to make all kinds of useful objects. But what if the same technology could be used to create human 1)＿＿＿＿＿＿＿? That is exactly what the French company Poietis is now doing. It has developed a bio-printer that is capable of printing three-2)＿＿＿＿＿＿ human tissue. First, it collects human cells from hospitals. Then, it mixes them with collagen to create "ink". Next, the laser in the printer lays spurts of "ink" in different locations to create 3D structures layer by layer. If we look at these cells under a 3)＿＿＿＿＿＿, we can see they are alive. Controlled by a predefined computer model, they start to 4)＿＿＿＿＿＿ with each other, and after a few days, a new epidermis begins to take shape.

PINPOINT

動名詞には、「主語」「補語」「動詞や前置詞の目的語」という 3 つの機能があります。

> （例）<u>Using</u> collagen as a material for the ink enables us to print human tissue.
> 　　　主語
> 　　The first step is <u>gathering</u> human cells to farm them.
> 　　　　　　　　　補語
> 　　By <u>following</u> the computer model, cells start <u>interacting</u> with each other.
> 　　　前置詞の目的語　　　　　　　　　　　　　　動詞の目的語

英文の空所に入る適切な語を枠内から選びましょう。

1. 3D printing is a process of ＿＿＿＿＿＿ three-dimensional physical objects based on a digital blueprint.

2. Once the printer starts printing, all you have to do is just ＿＿＿＿＿＿ until the whole process is completed.

3. A 3D-printer manufacturer is considering ＿＿＿＿＿＿ its market share by ＿＿＿＿＿＿ into the healthcare field.

expanding	waiting	making	moving

FURTHER INVESTIGATION

系統図（system diagram）は、関連する要素・概念を大きなものから小さなものに枝分かれさせながら網羅的に整理するものです。各要素の関連性の可視化や、不可欠な要素の欠落防止に有効です。

次の系統図は、医療分野における 3D プリンティングの活用方法を概略的にまとめたものです。図中の空所に入る活用方法を下記から選びましょう。

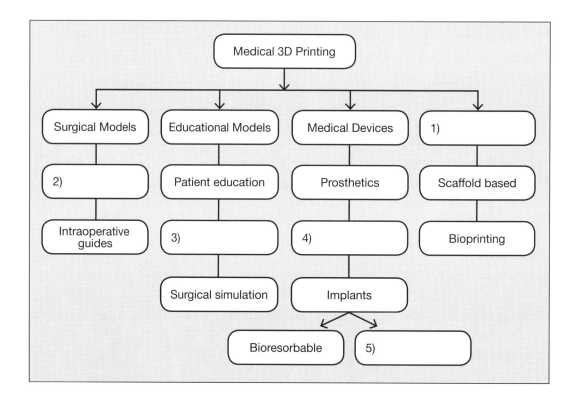

a. Wearable devices   b. Permanent   c. Learner education

d. Tissue Engineering   e. Preoperative planning

Caring for Strays

IC化する動物保護

トルコの大都会イスタンブールは、洋の東西が交錯する世界史上の要所。国際色豊かな人々が行きかうこの市街地には、飼い主のいない野良犬や猫もあふれています。その動物たちを IC タグで管理するシステムが市当局の出資で導入され、動物たちの健康管理だけでなく、人々の生活環境維持にも役立っています。

VOCABULARY
CD 2-02

A 次の語句に対応する日本語を選びましょう。

1. rabies　　　　　（　　）
2. parasitic　　　（　　）
3. identify　　　　（　　）
4. conscience　　（　　）
5. register　　　　（　　）

a. 寄生虫の
b. 登録する
c. 狂犬病
d. 特定する
e. 良心

B 次の語句の下線部と同じ発音が含まれる語を、A の語句から 1 つずつ選びましょう。

1. str<u>ay</u>「野良犬（猫）」　　　　　　　　　　　　　　　　　（　　）

2. city-sp<u>o</u>nsored veterinary bus「市が出資している獣医バス」　　（　　）

3. v<u>a</u>ccination「予防接種」　　　　　　　　　　　　　　　　（　　）

FINDING THE TOPIC
WEB動画　DVD

次の英文が映像の内容と合っている場合は T を、合っていない場合は F を選びましょう。

1. The veterinary bus is sponsored by residents of various districts in Istanbul.　　T / F

2. Municipal workers monitor animals using an electronic tagging system.　T / F

3. Istanbul's system has been successful in preventing new cases of rabies.　T / F

WEB動画 DVD CD 2-03

Ⓐ 音声を聴いて、空所に入る語を書き取りましょう。
Ⓑ スクリプトを読んで、内容を把握しましょう。

Mevlüde: local

Nihan Dinçer: Istanbul city veterinarian

Tugce Demirlek: Istanbul city head veterinarian

Umut Demir: Istanbul city veterinarian

Narrator: In Istanbul, it's raining cats and dogs. Turkey's cultural capital is home to 15 million human inhabitants, and tens of thousands of four-legged ¹( ). Far from being treated like pests, the animals are cared for by the authorities. 5 This city-sponsored ²( ) bus travels to different neighbourhoods, where residents bring homeless cats and dogs in need.

Mevlüde: He needed help. We saw that his eye was shut. We work on the campus and we often contact the town 10 hall when we see animals in need of treatment.

Nihan Dinçer: When these animals are unhealthy, some ³( ) illnesses can be transmitted to humans. So, keeping these animals healthy is actually keeping the people around them healthy, 15 which makes our work all the more important.

Narrator: More than 400 municipal workers, including 80 vets, are tasked with picking up poorly strays or those not yet ⁴( ), like this orphaned two-month-old puppy. The animal is treated with 20 antiparasitics and ⁵( ), then fitted with an electronic tag. If it needs more care, the vets will bring it to one of the city's six animal clinics.

Tugce Demirlek: We know all the dogs thanks to their tags. The 25 electronic tag system that I am showing you now,

inhabitant 住民

authorities 当局

transmit 感染する
municipal 自治体の
vet (=veterinarian) 獣医
poorly 元気がない
orphaned 親を失った

antiparasitic 駆虫薬

this is the device for reading them. Once we scan them, you can see the number here, and with the number we can find all the information we need to know about this dog on our database. 30

Narrator: And it's not only the sick who are looked after. Every day more than a ton of food is distributed to cats and dogs living in the wastelands surrounding the city. It's a way of staying on the packs' good side, but for locals, there's more to it than that. 35

distribute 配る

wasteland 荒れ地

pack 群れ

Umut Demir: In Turkey, because of our beliefs, we must be compassionate to other living beings. Their situation weighs on our ⁶(   ), so we cannot simply abandon these animals.

Narrator: Some 145,000 animals have been tagged and 40 ⁷(   ) by the city council and their team. Thanks to their monitoring system, not a single case of rabies has been reported in the city for three years.

compassionate 思いやり
を持つ
weigh on... 〜に重くのし
かかる
city council 市議会

COMPREHENSION

1 については質問に対する答えを、2 については下線部に入るものを選びましょう。

1. What does Istanbul NOT provide stray animals?
    (A) Food
    (B) Shelter
    (C) Medical care
    (D) Electronic tags

2. Our religious beliefs teach us that we must be _____ to other living beings.
    (A) compassionate
    (B) comforting
    (C) convenient
    (D) contented

次の英文は、スクリプトの要点をプレゼンテーションのスピーチ形式にまとめたものです。
音声を聴いて、空所に入る語句を記入しましょう。

The purpose of this presentation is to consider more humane ways to treat stray animals. Istanbul has tens of thousands of such animals. Rather than treating them like ₁)_____, the authorities care for them, using a veterinary bus that travels to different neighbourhoods. Residents bring homeless cats and dogs, which sometimes have parasitic illnesses that can be ₂)_____ to humans, so treating them keeps people healthy. ₃)_____ workers fit electronic tags to dogs, and information about them is stored in a database. The city also feeds the animals, delivering food every day to cats and dogs living in wastelands ₄)_____ the city. Authorities have tagged more than 145,000 animals. Thanks to this monitoring system, no cases of rabies have been reported in the last three years.

● *PINPOINT*

次のような概数を示す語句が名詞に先行する場合があります。不定冠詞 a が先行する場合と、
thousand などの数を示す語自体に複数形の s が付く場合では、意味が異なります。

(例) <u>a</u> thousand of Xs「千のX」	⇔ thousand<u>s</u> of Xs「数千のX」
<u>a</u> ten (of) thousands of Ys「１万のY」	⇔ ten<u>s</u> of thousands of Ys「数万のY」
<u>a</u> million of Zs「百万のZ」	⇔ million<u>s</u> of Zs「数百万のZ」
<u>a</u> ton of food「１トンの餌」	⇔ ton<u>s</u> of food「数トンの餌」

上記の表現と日本語を参考にして、英文の空所に入る語句を記入しましょう。

1. In Istanbul, _____ municipal workers are picking up poorly strays.

   「イスタンブールでは、数百人の自治体の職員が元気のない野良犬や猫を捕えています。」

2. The number of animal hospitals in Japan has been steadily increasing with about _____ hospitals operating in 2019.

   「日本における動物病院の数は堅調に増加していて、2019年には１万ほど病院が営業しています。」

FURTHER INVESTIGATION

折れ線グラフ（line graph）は、2つの変数の関係を可視化するもので、多くの場合、縦軸で数量を、横軸では時間の推移を表します。

次のグラフは、日本国内で保護された犬猫の数の推移を表したものです。下記の質問に答えましょう。

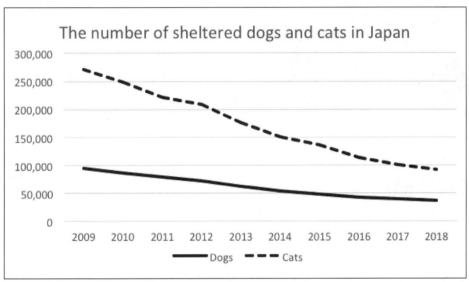

The number of sheltered dogs and cats in Japan

(Based on: https://www.env.go.jp/nature/dobutsu/aigo/2_data/statistics/dog-cat.html)

A 次の1～4に該当する英語を選びましょう。

1. 縦軸（＝Y軸）   (   )   a. solid line

2. 横軸（＝X軸）   (   )   b. broken line

3. 実線   (   )   c. horizontal axis

4. 破線   (   )   d. vertical axis

B 次の英文がグラフの内容と合っている場合はTを、合っていない場合はFを記入しましょう。

1. (   ) In Japan, the number of sheltered dogs has been decreasing year by year, and so has the number of sheltered cats.

2. (   ) Over the past 10 years, the number of sheltered cats has always been smaller than that of sheltered dogs.

Coal before Comfort

12 UNIT

鉄道敷設への腐心

急激な人口爆発が予測されるアフリカでは、それに対応するインフラ整備が急務。大陸南東部に位置するモザンビークでも、鉄道網の大規模な整備が計画中です。けれども主体となる国際企業の興味は、住民の生活環境改善というより、どうやら経済的利益の追求のようで…企業活動の建前と本音が鋭く交差しています。

VOCABULARY

🎧 2-06

A 次の語句に対応する日本語を選びましょう。

1. mineral wealth （　） a. 鉱物資源
2. coal mines （　） b. 継続
3. continuation （　） c. 複合企業
4. passenger traffic （　） d. 石炭鉱山
5. conglomerate （　） e. 旅客輸送

B 次の語句の下線部と同じ発音が含まれる語を、A の語句から 1 つずつ選びましょう。

1. public debt「公的債務」 （国や地方公共団体が抱えている債務残高） （　）

2. commercial operation「営業運転」 （　）

3. private capital「民間資本」 （個人や企業が保有している資本） （　）

FINDING THE TOPIC

WEB動画 🖥️ 📀 DVD

次の英文が映像の内容と合っている場合は T を、合っていない場合は F を選びましょう。

1. In Mozambique, the government is no longer in charge of rail development. T / F

2. The economic success of the line has made rail travel more comfortable for passengers. T / F

3. There is concern that the closure of coal mines will have a negative effect on rail operations. T / F

CHECKING THE SCRIPT

WEB動画 📺 DVD 🎞 CD 💿 2-07

A 音声を聴いて、空所に入る語を書き取りましょう。
B スクリプトを読んで、内容を把握しましょう。

Argentina Armando: rail passenger

Sergio Paunde: CDN spokesperson

Benjamin Pequenino: railway specialist

Narrator: It's three o'clock in the morning at Nampula Station in central Mozambique. Another overcrowded train, heading 350 kilometres towards Cuamba. It will be a suffocating journey of more than 10 hours, even for those who boarded early enough to get a ₅ seat.

Argentina Armando: We can't stand it anymore. There aren't enough carriages and there are too many people. The train is always full. There's not enough room.

Narrator: The Mozambique government has prioritised rail ₁₀ development in recent years. But mounting public ¹( ) forced the authorities to cede control of the project to the private sector. This line's operator, CDN, is owned by Brazilian mining giant Vale and Japanese ²( ) Mitsui. ₁₅ Since 2005, it has restored the former colonial line which linked its inland coal ³( ) with the port at Nacala. It now operates a network of 1,350 kilometres following an investment of more than 4 billion euros. ₂₀

Sergio Paunde: We've had very positive growth from 2016 to 2017. In terms of goods, we saw an increase of 65 percent. We carry 400,000 tonnes a year. And in terms of passenger ⁴( ), we've recorded the largest increase of 275 percent. ₂₅

Narrator: But economic success has not translated into increased comfort for passengers since the

Nampula ナンプラ (モザンビーク第三の都市)
Cuamba クアンバ (モザンビークの都市)
suffocating journey 息の詰まるような旅
board 乗車する

carriage 客車
prioritise 優先する

mounting 増大する
cede 譲渡する
private sector 民間
CDN (= Northern Development Corridor) 北部回廊開発

mining giant Vale 巨大鉱業企業であるヴァーレ社
Mitsui 三井物産株式会社
colonial line 植民地時代の路線
inland 内陸の
Nacala ナカラ (モザンビークの都市)
in terms of... ～の観点では
translate into... ～に形を変える

company's focus is on its more profitable 5( ) operation.

Benjamin Pequenino: Today, the Nacala line only exists because of coal. But once the mine is closed, what will justify the 6( ) of operations?

Narrator: Eight new 'rail corridor' projects are now underway in Mozambique, all funded with the private 7( ) of large companies, attracted by the country's vast mineral wealth. Yet whether their interest in the sector will continue for the long-haul is as yet unclear.

profitable 利益になる

30

justify 正当化する

rail corridor 鉄道路線

fund 資金提供する

35

for the long-haul 長期にわたって
as yet 今のところは

COMPREHENSION

1 については質問に対する答えを、2 については下線部に入るものを選びましょう。

1. What is the main source of the rail company's income?
   (A) Passenger fares
   (B) Carrying freight
   (C) Government funds
   (D) The stock market

2. In terms of goods, the company _____ an increase of 65 percent between 2016 and 2017.
   (A) accepted
   (B) provided
   (C) saw
   (D) took

● *PRESENTING THE CONTENTS*

次の英文は、スクリプトの要点をプレゼンテーションのスピーチ形式にまとめたものです。
音声を聴いて、空所に入る語句を記入しましょう。

Investment in public transportation is vital everywhere, particularly in developing countries with a growing population. However, if the private sector is responsible for this, can we be sure it truly has the public interest at heart? Recently, the government of Mozambique has 1)_____ rail development but mounting public debt forced it to cede control to the private sector. The companies involved restored an old 2)_____ line linking coal mines to a port. The venture has been commercially successful, with large growth in 3)_____ and passenger numbers. But since the company prioritises its more profitable freight operation, this economic success has not increased passengers' comfort. This line only exists because of the coal it carries. People worry there will be nothing to 4)_____ operating costs once the coal mines have closed.

● *PINPOINT*

数量の増減を示す表現の一つに、"主語＋動詞＋目的語（increase / decrease など増減を示す名詞を含む）"の構文があります。この構文の 主語 は we / the year / this study などで、一方、動詞には see / find などが多用されます。また、目的語には「前置詞 of ＋ X（増減の数量）」や「前置詞 in ＋ Y（増減している項目・内容）」が後続する場合があります。

（例）In 2017, we saw an increase **of** 275% **in** the number of passengers.
「2017年に、旅客数が275%増加した。」

[ ] 内の語句を適切な語順に並べかえ、英文を完成させましょう。

1. The year 2017 _____ the population of Mozambique from the previous year.

    [in / saw / of about 1.0% / an increase]

2. The nation has _____ the past 10 years.

    [over / a steady rise / in its GDP / seen]

3. A survey _____ the 2018 trade balance of Mozambique.

    [in / a decrease / found / of $973 million]

FURTHER INVESTIGATION

> 米国中央情報局（CIA）が公開している *The World Factbook* は、世界中の 268 の国・地域に関する主要な情報（政治・経済・交通・地理など）を年鑑形式でまとめた情報源です。

次の枠内は、The World Factbook に収録されているモザンビークに関する情報の一部です。下記の 1 ～ 4 が内容と合っている場合は T を、合っていない場合は F を選びましょう。

Economy
Overview: At independence in 1975, Mozambique was one of the world's poorest countries. Socialist policies, economic mismanagement, and a brutal civil war from 1977 to 1992 further impoverished the country. In 1987, the government embarked on a series of macroeconomic reforms designed to stabilize the economy. These steps, combined with donor assistance and with political stability since the multi-party elections in 1994, propelled the country's GDP, in purchasing power parity terms, from $4 billion in 1993 to about $37 billion in 2017.
Transportation
Airports—with paved runways: total: 21 (2017)
Airports—with unpaved runways: total: 77 (2013)
Railways: total: 4,787 km (2014)
Roadways: total: 31,083 km (2015) paved: 7,365 km (2015) unpaved: 23,718 km (2015)
Waterways: 460 km (2010)

(Based on: https://www.cia.gov/library/publications/the-world-factbook/geos/mz.html)

1. The Mozambique government started to reform the country's economy in 1990s.   T / F

2. The country saw a large increase of almost $33 billion in its GDP from 1993 to 2017.   T / F

3. The total length of railways is more than 10 times longer than that of waterways.   T / F

4. The total length of paved roadways is nearly a quarter of that of unpaved roadways.   T / F

Lifesaving Lake

感染を防ぐ命の水

感染症予防の最善の方策は、手洗いとうがい。その
ために必須なのは、水です。水道網が未整備の地域
では、湖や川が主要な生命線。コンゴとルワンダの
国境にあるキブ湖は、まさにその重責を担う湖です。
パンデミック（爆発的な大流行）を防ぐという意味で
は、"世界を救う根源の水"と言えるかもしれません。

VOCABULARY

🎧 2-10

A 次の語句に対応する日本語を選びましょう。

1. populate （　　） a. 配送する
2. pump （　　） b. くみ上げる
3. spread （　　） c. ～に頼る
4. rely on... （　　） d. （感染が）拡大する、（感染）拡大
5. distribute （　　） e. 居住させる

B 次の語句の下線部と同じ発音が含まれる語を、A の語句から 1 つずつ選びましょう。

1. Ebola response team 「エボラ出血熱対策チーム」 （　　）

2. water distribution network 「配水管網」 （　　）

3. entrepreneurial water supplier 「起業精神のある給水業者」 （　　）

FINDING THE TOPIC

WEB動画 / DVD

次の英文が映像の内容と合っている場合は T を、合っていない場合は F を選びましょう。

1. Without water, it would be impossible to prevent the spread of Ebola. T / F

2. Goma's water distribution network pumps water directly from Lake Kivu. T / F

3. Goma's Ebola response teams usually get water from Rwanda as well as from Lake Kivu. T / F

CHECKING THE SCRIPT

WEB動画 ▢📱 DVD 💿 CD 💿 2-11

A 音声を聴いて、空所に入る語を書き取りましょう。
B スクリプトを読んで、内容を把握しましょう。

Jean Nepo: supervisor of the response against Ebola at the public port of Goma

Aimé Bahati: drinking water supplier

Jacques Sinzahera: pro-democracy activist

Narrator: The golden rule to avoid the spread of Ebola is to wash your hands regularly. But for that, you need water. In Goma, in the Democratic Republic of Congo, water is essential in the fight against the virus ¹( ) across the region. ₅ Facing shortages, Ebola response teams have had to ²( ) on the generosity of Lake Kivu to supply health checkpoints.

Jean Nepo: The lake is crucial because it helps vulnerable people, poor people, and it helps in the fight ₁₀ against Ebola. When water is abundant, we can help prevent the spread of the disease.

Narrator: Finding water in Goma is difficult. The city's water distribution ³( ) is outdated and only supplies a few neighbourhoods. For many ₁₅ of Goma's inhabitants, access to water means ⁴( ) it directly from the lake.

Aimé Bahati: The water problem in Goma clearly shows that only this part of the city is supplied, not the whole city. That's why a lot of people come to the lake to ₂₀ get their water. They also then carry some home for those who need it.

Narrator: On a daily basis, entrepreneurial water ⁵( ) organise several trips. The lake water is treated with chlorine and then ₂₅ ⁶( ) to reservoirs in the region. Water towers like these require 5,000 litres of water

golden rule 黄金律

Goma ゴマ（コンゴ東部の都市）

generosity 恵み
Lake Kivu キブ湖

vulnerable （ウイルスに）弱い
outdated 旧式の

trip 移送
chlorine 塩素
reservoir 貯水タンク

62

per day.

Jacques Sinzahera: If the lake wasn't there, it would be catastrophic. Maybe the response teams would get 30 water from elsewhere, maybe in Rwanda, in Sake. But it would be catastrophic. We would not even survive. We wouldn't survive because the lake is our only source of drinking water.

Narrator: Lake Kivu is an essential force in stopping the 35 spread of Ebola, and an invaluable resource for the local [7]( ). For the people that live on its shores, the waters of Kivu give, shape, and preserve life.

Rwanda ルワンダ
Sake サケ（ルワンダ東部のサケ湖畔にある都市）

● *COMPREHENSION*

1 については質問に対する答えを、2 については下線部に入るものを選びましょう。

1. What is true of the water supply in Goma?
   (A) It is too expensive for most people.
   (B) It comes entirely from neighbouring countries.
   (C) It does not reach every part of the city.
   (D) It is dirty and causes disease.

2. For many people, the lake is their only _____ of drinking water.
   (A) source
   (B) cause
   (C) method
   (D) type

次の英文は、スクリプトの要点をプレゼンテーションのスピーチ形式にまとめたものです。
音声を聴いて、空所に入る語句を記入しましょう。

Regular hand washing helps prevent the spread of Ebola and so water is 1)_____. In Goma, in the Democratic Republic of Congo, Ebola response teams have had to rely on water from Lake Kivu because of water shortages. The city's water 2)_____ network is outdated and only supplies a few neighbourhoods. Many inhabitants have to pump water directly from the lake. Many people come to the lake to get their water and then carry some home for those who need it. Entrepreneurial water suppliers make several trips. They treat the lake water with chlorine and then distribute it to 3)_____ in the region. Lake Kivu is essential in stopping the spread of Ebola and an 4)_____ resource for local people. I'd like to close my presentation there. I hope I've been able to bring it to a successful conclusion.

● **PINPOINT**

副詞句 "on a X basis" は、"X" に入る語によってさまざまな意味に変化します。

（例）	・on a daily basis「日常的に」	・on a commercial basis「商業ベースで」
	・on a trial basis「試験的に」	・on a voluntary basis「自主的に」
	・on a national basis「全国的に」	・on an interim basis「暫定的に」

次の日本語の空所を埋めましょう。

1. The doctors provided medical treatment for patients on a regular basis.
   「医者たちは_____に患者に対して医療を提供した。」

2. Some of the members engage in this mission on a full-time basis.
   「メンバーの中にはこの任務に_____で従事している人もいる。」

3. The monthly number of patients is compiled on a regional basis.
   「毎月の患者数は_____に集計される。」

FURTHER INVESTIGATION

イラストレーション（illustration）は、複雑かつ場合によっては専門的な内容を容易に伝えるために使用される視覚情報（visuals）の一つです。

次のイラストレーションは、エボラ出血熱が感染する経路の説明です。イラストを参考にして、英文の空所に入る適切な語を下記から選びましょう。

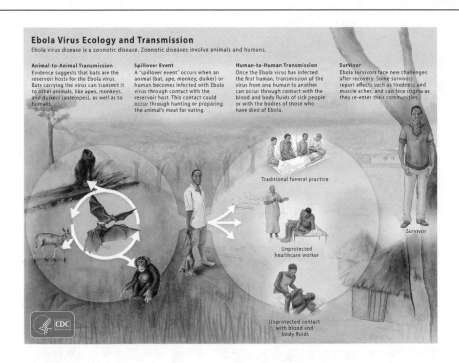

Ebola Virus Ecology and Transmission
Ebola virus disease is a zoonotic disease. Zoonotic diseases involve animals and humans.

Animal-to-Animal Transmission
Evidence suggests that bats are the reservoir hosts for the Ebola virus. Bats carrying the virus can transmit it to other animals, like apes, monkeys, and duikers (antelopes), as well as to humans.

Spillover Event
A "spillover event" occurs when an animal (bat, ape, monkey, duiker) or human becomes infected with Ebola virus through contact with the reservoir host. This contact could occur through hunting or preparing the animal's meat for eating.

Human-to-Human Transmission
Once the Ebola virus has infected the first human, transmission of the virus from one human to another can occur through contact with the blood and body fluids of sick people or with the bodies of those who have died of Ebola.

Survivor
Ebola survivors face new challenges after recovery. Some survivors report effects such as tiredness and muscle aches, and can face stigma as they re-enter their communities.

Traditional funeral practice

Unprotected healthcare worker

Unprotected contact with blood and body fluids

Survivor

CDC

Ebola virus disease (EVD) is a deadly disease with occasional outbreaks that occur primarily on the African continent. EVD most commonly affects people and nonhuman primates, such as monkeys, gorillas, and chimpanzees.

Ebola virus was first discovered in 1976 near the Ebola River in what is now the Democratic Republic of Congo. Since then, the virus has been infecting people from time to time, leading to (1:　　　　　) in several African countries. Scientists do not know where Ebola virus comes from. However, based on the nature of similar viruses, they believe the virus is animal-borne, with (2:　　　　　) or nonhuman primates being the most likely source.

The virus spreads to people initially through direct contact with the blood, body fluids and tissues of (3:　　　　　). Ebola virus then spreads to other (4:　　　　　) through direct contact with body fluids of a person who is sick with or has died from EVD.

(Source: https://www.cdc.gov/vhf/ebola/about.html)

a. people	b. bats	c. outbreaks	d. animals

Saving a Wooden Giant

欧州最大の木造建築

木造建築は、日本が誇る高度な建築技術の一つ。1,300 年以上前に建てられた奈良の法隆寺は、世界最古とされています。その 10 分の 1 にも満たない歴史しかありませんが、トルコのビュユック島に欧州最大の木造建築物があります。石造が主流の地で、崩壊寸前のこの建物にはどのような運命が待ち構えているのでしょうか。

VOCABULARY　　　　2-14

A 次の語句に対応する日本語を選びましょう。

1. assess 　　（　　）　　　　a. 腐敗する
2. deteriorate 　（　　）　　　　b. 修復する
3. rot 　　　（　　）　　　　c. 査定する
4. restore 　　（　　）　　　　d. 置き去りにする
5. abandon 　　（　　）　　　　e. 悪化する

B 次の語句の下線部と同じ発音が含まれる語を、A の語句から 1 つずつ選びましょう。

1. coll<u>a</u>pse 「崩壊」　　　　　　　　　　　　　　　　　　　　（　　）

2. <u>or</u>phanage 「児童養護施設」　　　　　　　　　　　　　　　　（　　）

3. Europe's seven most end<u>a</u>ngered sites 「欧州七大危機遺産」　（　　）

FINDING THE TOPIC　　　　WEB動画　DVD

次の英文が映像の内容と合っている場合は T を、合っていない場合は F を選びましょう。

1. Construction of the building was completed in 1964.　　　　　　T / F

2. The building was first a luxury hotel, then a church, and finally an orphanage.　　　　　　T / F

3. The experts would prefer not to rebuild the structure.　　　　　T / F

● CHECKING THE SCRIPT

WEB動画 DVD CD 2-15

Ａ 音声を聴いて、空所に入る語を書き取りましょう。
Ｂ スクリプトを読んで、内容を把握しましょう。

Erol Baytas: caretaker

Burçin Altinsay: Europa Nostra Turkey

Apostolos Poridis: architect and head of the Technical Office at the Ecumenical Patriarchate of Constantinople

Narrator: It takes an hour by boat from Istanbul to reach the largest of the Princes' Islands. On a hilltop is this huge historic building that has fallen into ruins. Twenty-thousand square metres of wood [is] ¹(   ) to the elements. Erol ₅ is the caretaker of this former orphanage, which closed in 1964. He says it is on the verge of ²(   ), so it's been closed to try and save the building.

the Princes' Islands プリンス諸島（トルコのイスタンブール沖の群島）
the elements 雨風
on the verge of... 〜の寸前で

Erol Baytas: Of course, my job as a caretaker has become much ₁₀ more difficult because every day many people come. Everyone is curious. It's a big building. People come from all over the world after hearing about it.

Narrator: Built in 1898 by a French architect, the building ₁₅ overlooks the Marmara Sea and was intended to be a luxury hotel. In the end, however, the Greek Orthodox Church transformed it into an ³(   ), through which more than 5,000 children passed. Today, it's classified among ₂₀ Europe's seven most ⁴(   ) sites by heritage organisation Europa Nostra, which hopes to save it.

the Marmara Sea マルマラ海（トルコ北西部の内海）

the Greek Orthodox Church ギリシア正教会

Europa Nostra ヨーロッパ・ノストラ（欧州の文化・自然遺産保護団体の連盟）

Burçin Altinsay: We believe it is the largest wooden building in Europe. Its historical characteristics, the details, ₂₅ distinguish it from other constructions. For all these reasons, it occupies an important place in the history of this place, but also for the Greek minority.

Narrator: This summer, a delegation of experts will come to ⁵(   ) what can be done with the ₃₀ building, and what the cost of renovations would be. The idea is to try to rehabilitate it without having to rebuild it.

Apostolos Porídis: The main structure is solid. The big problem comes from the roof. But the big advantage is that ₃₅ the building is so high that it dries out. When it takes on water, it dries with the wind, so there is no ⁶(   ). But from what I've seen, the north face has been badly damaged.

Narrator: With every season, the condition of this neglected ₄₀ building deteriorates even further. Europa Nostra hopes that urgent ⁷(   ) work can begin before next winter.

Greek minority 少数派のギリシア人

delegation 代表団

renovation 改築

main structure 主要構造

● COMPREHENSION

1 については質問に対する答えを、2 については下線部に入るものを選びましょう。

1. What is one factor that might make it easier to conserve the building?
   (A) It is easy to be dried out.
   (B) It does not get wet.
   (C) It gets only a few visitors.
   (D) It is fine except for its north face.

2. The building _____ the Marmara Sea.
   (A) oversees
   (B) overlooks
   (C) overturns
   (D) overhangs

● PRESENTING THE CONTENTS 2-16

次の英文は、スクリプトの要点をプレゼンテーションのスピーチ形式にまとめたものです。
音声を聴いて、空所に入る語句を記入しましょう。

A good example to illustrate the problems of historical renovation is a huge building near Istanbul that is on the 1)＿＿＿＿＿＿＿ of collapse. It was built in 1898 and was intended to be a luxury hotel. In the end, it was 2)＿＿＿＿＿＿＿ into an orphanage. Today, it is classified as an endangered site. Some believe it is the largest wooden building in Europe. A delegation of experts will come to assess what can be done with the building. The key point here is to 3)＿＿＿＿＿＿＿ it without having to rebuild it. The big problem comes from the roof, but the big advantage is that the building is high, and so when it takes on water, the wind dries it out and there is no 4)＿＿＿＿＿＿＿.

● PINPOINT

関係代名詞 "what" は名詞節を作ります。

（例）This summer, they will come to assess what can be done with the building.
「この夏、彼らはこの建物に対して何ができるのかを査定しにやって来ます。」

日本語を参考にして、[　]内の語句を適切な語順に並べかえ、英文を完成させましょう。

1. What ＿＿＿＿＿＿＿＿＿＿＿＿＿＿＿＿＿＿＿＿＿ that it was
   intended to be a hotel.
   [this building / most interesting / about / is / is]
   「この建物について最も興味深いことは、それがホテルになる予定だったことである。」

2. A group of experts are due ＿＿＿＿＿＿＿＿＿＿＿＿＿＿＿
   would be.
   [what / of / to estimate / renovations / the cost]
   「専門家の集団が、改築費用はどのくらいになるのかを見積もる予定である。」

3. The architect was surprised ＿＿＿＿＿＿＿＿＿＿＿＿＿＿＿
   of the building.
   [what / he found / the examination / at / during]
   「その建築家は、この建物の調査中に発見したことに驚いた。」

次のランキング表は、世界に現存する木造建築物を高さの順で10位まで一覧にしたものです。
下記の英文の空所に入る適切な語句を記入しましょう。

The top 10 tallest wooden buildings existing in the world

Rank	Name	Height (m)	Location	Completion
1	Gliwice Radio Tower	118	Gliwice, Poland	1935
2	Sanctuary of Truth	105	Pattaya, Thailand	To be completed until 2025
3	Dushan Shuisi Building	99.9	Dushan County, China	2019
4	Mjøstårnet	85.4	Brumunddal, Norway	2019
5	Săpânța-Peri Church	78	Săpânța, Romania	1997
6	Yongding Pagoda	69.7	Beijing, China	2011
7	Pagoda of Fogong Temple	67.3	Ying County, China	1056
8	Ieud Monastery	60	Ieud, Romania	2003
9	Rozavlea-Șesu Mănăstirii	58	Rozavlea, Romania	2017
10	Bârsana Monastery	57	Bârsana, Romania	1995

1. To be precise, the world's tallest structure in the table is a _____ rather than a building.

2. Four of the top 10 tallest buildings can be found in _____ _____.

3. Construction work of the building named _____ is scheduled to continue until 2025.

4. The oldest wooden building in the table is _____ in China.

5. _____ of the top 10 buildings are over 100 metres high.

Protecting an Ancient City

UNIT 15

古代文明の新たな敵

モヘンジョダロは、4,000年ほど前に栄えたインダス文明（Indus [Valley] Civilisation）最大級の都市。世界各地の遺跡と同様に、長年の風化で当時の先端的都市開拓の名残が失われつつあります。ユネスコなど国際機関の努力や、観光客を含む一人一人の心がけで、人類史を掘り下げる第一級資料を後世に引き継ぐことができるでしょうか。

VOCABULARY

CD 2-18

A 次の語句に対応する日本語を選びましょう。

1. decline （　）
2. excavate （　）
3. preserve （　）
4. gutter （　）
5. expose （　）

a. 発掘する
b. 側溝
c. （日光・風雨などに）さらす
d. 衰退する
e. 保存する

B 次の語句の下線部と同じ発音が含まれる語を、Aの語句から1つずつ選びましょう。

1. UNESCO's World Heritage List「ユネスコの世界遺産一覧」　（　）

2. flush toilet「水洗トイレ」　（　）

3. Mesopotamia「メソポタミア」　（　）
（ティグリス川とユーフラテス川の流域［あるいはそこで栄えた古代文明］）

FINDING THE TOPIC

WEB動画 / DVD

次の英文が映像の内容と合っている場合はTを、合っていない場合はFを選びましょう。

1. Mohenjo Daro is the only site in Pakistan that appears on UNESCO's World Heritage List.　T / F

2. It is possible that Indus Civilisation is even older than ancient Egyptian Civilisation.　T / F

3. Excavating the ancient city could expose it to many kinds of potential damage.　T / F

71

CHECKING THE SCRIPT

WEB動画 DVD CD 2-19

A 音声を聴いて、空所に入る語を書き取りましょう。
B スクリプトを読んで、内容を把握しましょう。

Michael Jansen: German archaeologist and expert on the Indus Civilisation

Jonathan Mark Kenoyer: professor of anthropology at University of Wisconsin

Richard Meadow: senior lecturer of anthropology at Harvard University

Narrator: The ruins of a once great city. Mohenjo Daro was built by the ancient Indus Civilisation, which could predate Egypt's pharaohs. Lying on the banks of the Indus River, it's one of six sites in Pakistan that feature on UNESCO's World ¹( ) List. A team of international archaeologists is now seeking to safeguard it. 5

Michael Jansen: Everybody knows Egypt. Nobody knows Mohenjo Daro and the Indus Civilisation. This has to be changed. 10

Narrator: The Indus Valley Civilisation could have numbered up to 5 million people, with Mohenjo Daro its largest and most advanced settlement. Houses had their own wells, tiled bathrooms and ²( ) toilets. The city's avenues 15 boasted drains, ³( ) and containers for waste disposal. At the center of it all, one of the key buildings: a massive public bath.

Jonathan Mark Kenoyer: Indus cities were organised in a way which has much more, I would say, equality among 20 citizens. In Mesopotamia, the streets went from the city to the palace or the city gateway to the temple whereas, in Harappan cities, all the streets were organised to allow access to the whole city.

Narrator: ⁴( ) all this heritage is a great 25 challenge. Only a small portion of the site has been ⁵( ) properly, and there are

---

ruin 遺跡
predate 以前にさかのぼる
pharaoh ファラオ（古代エジプトの君主の称号）
feature 登場する
archaeologist 考古学者

safeguard 保護する

number 達する
up to... ～にまで
settlement 開拓地
tiled タイル張りの

boast 誇る

waste disposal ごみ処理

public bath 公衆浴場

Harappan ハラッパの（モヘンジョ・ダロと並ぶインダス文明の代表的都市遺跡）
portion 一部

currently no plans to dig any further.

dig 発掘する

Richard Meadow: It's being actually preserved when it is buried. Once you ⁶(   ) it, there's all sorts 30 of different forces which affect it. So, the weather, the nature of the environment around, how well-behaved the people who visit the site…

Narrator: Tourists and locals have left their mark, damaging areas of the site. Heat, insecurity and salt from the 35 underground water table pose additional threats. To this day, no one knows why the Indus Civilisation ⁷(   ) some 19 centuries before Christ, and the answer may lie below ground. But for now, the priority remains to protect what has 40 been found before digging for more treasures.

well-behaved 行儀良くふるまって
local 地元の人
water table 地下水面
pose 突きつける
to this day 今日まで

● COMPREHENSION

1 については質問に対する答えを、2 については下線部に入るものを選びましょう。

1. What is a source of danger that Mohenjo Daro does NOT face?
   (A) The behaviour of tourists and visitors
   (B) Weather conditions
   (C) Environmental threats
   (D) People stealing treasures

2. In Mesopotamia, streets went from the city to the palace _____, in Indus cities, the streets allowed access to the whole city.
   (A) whereas
   (B) however
   (C) when
   (D) therefore

PRESENTING THE CONTENTS

2-20

次の英文は、スクリプトの要点をプレゼンテーションのスピーチ形式にまとめたものです。
音声を聴いて、空所に入る語句を記入しましょう。

It is always exciting when archeologists discover a site that can increase our
knowledge of history and civilisation. Such discoveries, however, can have
unfortunate consequences as excavating sites may 1)＿＿＿＿＿＿＿＿＿＿
them to threats. One such site is Mohenjo Daro in Pakistan, an ancient city
of the Indus Civilisation, which may be even older than Ancient Egypt.
Archeologists excavating the ancient city cite several dangers, including
the 2)＿＿＿＿＿＿＿＿＿＿ of visitors, weather conditions, and environmental
factors such as heat and salt from the underground water table. Only a
small 3)＿＿＿＿＿＿＿＿＿＿ of the site has therefore been excavated and
no further digging is planned. The archeologists' main priority is to
4)＿＿＿＿＿＿＿＿＿＿ what has so far been found, no matter what other
treasures may still lie buried.

PINPOINT

「対照」を示すさまざまな表現を用いて2つの物事を対置させることにより、読み手に分かり
やすい対比構造を作ることができます。

（例） In Mesopotamia, the streets went from the city to the palace **whereas**, in
Harappan cities, all the streets were organised to allow access to the whole
city.
「メソポタミアでは、街道は都市から王宮へと走っていました。**ところが**ハラッパ
の都市では、すべての街道が都市全体に行くことを可能にするよう配置されてい
たのです。」

日本語を参考にして、英文の空所に入る適切な語句を枠内から選びましょう。

1. Everybody knows Egypt, ＿＿＿＿＿＿＿＿ few knows Mohenjo Daro.
   「誰もがエジプトを知っていますが、一方でモヘンジョダロについてはほとんど誰も知りません。」

2. ＿＿＿＿＿＿＿＿ its prosperity, the Indus Civilisation declined some 19
   centuries before Christ.
   「繁栄していたにもかかわらず、インダス文明は紀元前19世紀のある時期に衰退しました。」

while	in spite of

74

● *FURTHER INVESTIGATION*

各種の申請（application）を行う際は，申請書（application form）提出上の注意に従い、遺漏なく必要書類を整えて提出することが重要です。

次の英文は，遺跡の発掘に係る申請書を記入・提出する際の注意事項です。下記の１〜４が注意事項の内容と合っている場合はＴを、合っていない場合はＦを選びましょう。

— Information and Advice Notes —

APPLICANTS ARE REQUESTED TO READ THESE BEFORE COMPLETING THE APPLICATION FORM AND IT WILL BE ASSUMED THAT THEY HAVE DONE SO.

1. The application form must be accompanied by a detailed method statement and a letter from the person or body funding this excavation, confirming that sufficient funds and other facilities are available to complete the archaeological excavation, post-excavation, and preliminary and final reports.

2. The completed application form, together with the detailed method statement and letter must be received by the National Monuments Service at least three weeks prior to the date on which it is proposed to commence the excavation. Note that, while the Service endeavours to process all applications as quickly as reasonable and has a general target of deciding on applications three weeks after receipt, no guarantee can be provided that this will be met and there is no legal entitlement on the part of an applicant to receive a decision on their application within three weeks.

3. Given that appropriate professional competence and experience is a material factor in deciding whether or not a licence should be issued, a first-time applicant may expect to be requested to attend an interview arranged by the Service to assess such competence and experience.

(Based on: https://www.archaeology.ie/licences/archaeological-excavation)

---

1. 申請書には、詳細な発掘方法の記述と、発掘費用の出資者／団体からの手紙が添付されている必要がある。　　　　　　　　　　　　　　　　　　　　　T / F

2. 発掘や発掘後の作業を始めるための十分な資金があるかどうかや、他施設が利用可能かどうかを確認しておく必要がある。　　　　　　　　　　　　　　T / F

3. 書類に不備があった場合には、修正した申請書を発掘開始から３週間以内に再提出する必要がある。　　　　　　　　　　　　　　　　　　　　　　　T / F

4. 発掘には専門性や経験が必要とされるため、申請者は面談される場合がある。　　T / F

Disappearing Island

島を削る温暖化の波

温暖化による海面上昇—この因果関係を否定する人々も存在しますが、水位上昇に脅かされる沿岸地域があることは厳然たる事実。影響が顕著なのは、海に囲まれた小さな島。米国ワシントン DC にほど近い面積わずか 3.2 km² のタンジア島は、かつて海に没したとされるアトランティス伝説の現代版になってしまうかも…。

VOCABULARY

🎵 CD 2-22

A 次の語句に対応する日本語を選びましょう。

1. erosion （　　）
2. flooding （　　）
3. accelerate （　　）
4. exacerbate （　　）
5. breakwall （　　）

a. 悪化させる
b. 加速する
c. 洪水
d. 防波堤
e. 浸食

B 次の語句の下線部と同じ発音が含まれる語を、A の語句から 1 つずつ選びましょう。

1. gl<u>o</u>bal warming「地球温暖化」 （　　）

2. bureaucr<u>a</u>tic delay「お役所仕事の遅れ」 （　　）

3. dr<u>e</u>dged sand「浚渫土（しゅんせつど）」
　（海底や川底を掘削することで発生する土砂やへどろ） （　　）

FINDING THE TOPIC

WEB動画 💻 DVD 🎵

次の英文が映像の内容と合っている場合は T を、合っていない場合は F を選びましょう。

1. Scientists predict that the island of Tangier will disappear before the end of the 21st century.　　　　T / F

2. Some residents do not believe that global climate change is making the situation worse.　　　　T / F

3. A new harbor was planned to be built in 2018.　　　　T / F

CHECKING THE SCRIPT

WEB動画 DVD CD 2-23

A 音声を聴いて、空所に入る語を書き取りましょう。
B スクリプトを読んで、内容を把握しましょう。

William Eskridge: fisherman

Dave Schulte: marine biologist

Carol Pruitt Moore: local resident

Narrator: William's family has lived on Tangier Island for the past 200 years, but his generation might be the last to see out their days here. This island on the east coast of the U.S. is slowly disappearing. Scientists predict that [1]( ) and rising 5 waters will wipe Tangier from the map over the next 40 years.

Tangier Island タンジア島
（米国バージニア州）

see out 最後まで見届ける

rising waters 海面上昇
wipe 消し去る

William Eskridge: I'd say at least 100 feet that has come in, that has took [→taken] the land away, just erosion, and it just seems like it's getting worst [→worse] every 10 year. I'm just kind of fearful [of] what it's going to be down the road. I mean, just a few short years.

Narrator: Erosion isn't a new phenomenon on Tangier. This deserted patch of land was once a village.

kind of ちょっと
down the road 今後
deserted さびれた
patch of land 土地の一角

Dave Schulte: 1876 to 1913.

15

Narrator: Now a few broken tombstones are all that is left. The island is only about a third of the size it was in the 1950s. But the author of a report on the shrinking island says there's no doubt that global warming is [2]( ) the problem.

20

tombstone 墓石

shrink 縮小する

number 人口

Dave Schulte: We, as people, don't like to believe we can really do something that bad to the world around us. But we can, you know — our technology, our numbers, the amount of carbon we're producing and putting into the atmosphere. We are changing the weather 25 now.

Narrator: ³(   ) is becoming more frequent. The rate of erosion is ⁴(   ). Yet, residents, many fervent Donald Trump supporters, still have a hard time believing that global ⁵(   ) is making things worse.

Carol Pruitt Moore: I do believe erosion is the main problem on Tangier. You know, some people say it's climate change and rise in sea level. I don't know that I believe that.

Narrator: After years of bureaucratic ⁶(   ), a breakwall is expected to be built in 2018 to help protect the harbor. But several other breakers, along with seawalls, and rebuilding parts of the island with ⁷(   ) sand will be needed in order to save Tangier — a plan that would cost tens of millions of dollars.

rate 速度

fervent 熱烈な

Donald Trump ドナルド・トランプ（米国45代大統領）

breaker 防波堤

seawall 護岸

● COMPREHENSION

1 については質問に対する答えを、2 については下線部に入るものを選びましょう。

1. What do residents believe is the main problem on the island?
    (A) Global warming
    (B) Erosion
    (C) Flooding
    (D) Rising sea levels

2. A breakwall is expected ＿＿＿＿＿ in 2018.
    (A) to build
    (B) building
    (C) be built
    (D) to be built

● *PRESENTING THE CONTENTS*

🎧 2-24

次の英文は、スクリプトの要点をプレゼンテーションのスピーチ形式にまとめたものです。
音声を聴いて、空所に入る語句を記入しましょう。

The greatest danger we currently face is climate change, and we must act before it is too late. However, some people deny climate change exists even when they see evidence of it with their own eyes. One example is the island of Tangier in the U.S., which is slowly 1)_____. Scientists predict that 2)_____ waters will wipe it from the map over the next 40 years. The island is now one-third of the size it was in the 1950s. It seems clear that global warming is 3)_____ the crisis. However, many residents fervently support President Donald Trump and deny that global warming plays a part, stating that the problem is simply 4)_____. There are plans to build a breakwall to protect the harbor, but this will probably not be enough to save the island.

● *PINPOINT*

特定の「動詞」（expect / design / intend / require など）は、"主語＋ be ＋「動詞」の過去分詞＋ to do" の構文で使用されます。その場合、"主語が do する" という中心的内容に対して、それぞれの「動詞」が持つ意味合いが追加されます。

（例）　・A breakwall **is expected to** be built in 2018.
　　　「2018年に防波堤が建設されることが**期待（予定）されている**。」
　　　（＝"防波堤が建設される"＋「期待（予定）されている」）

日本語を参考にして、英文の空所に入る語句を枠内から選び、必要なら形をかえて記入しましょう。

1. These devices _____ be carried under water.
  「この機器は、水中で携帯できるように設計されている。」

2. The average temperature in 2020 _____ be slightly higher than before.
  「2020年の平均気温は、以前よりわずかに高くなる見込みである。」

3. Each of us _____ fight climate change.
  「私たちのそれぞれが気候変動に対処することが求められている。」

be expected to	be required to	be designed to

FURTHER INVESTIGATION

各種の報告書（report）は、視覚情報（visuals）と文字情報を的確に組み合わせながら、過不足のない記述を行うことが重要です。

次のグラフと英文は、IPCC（Intergovernmental Panel on Climate Change、国連気候変動に関する政府間パネル）による地球上の海水面の上昇に関する報告書からの抜粋です。英文の空所に入る適切な語を下記から選びましょう。

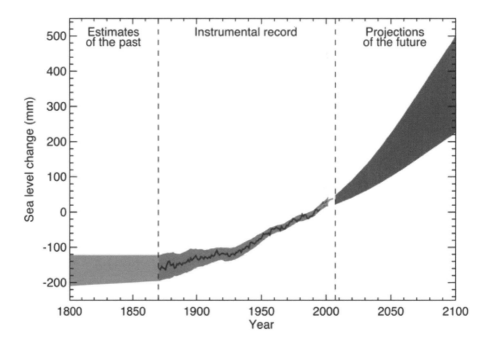

For the period before 1870, global measurements of sea level are not available. The grey shading in the left column shows the uncertainty in the (1:   ) long-term rate of sea level change. The line in the middle area is a reconstruction of global mean sea level from tide gauges, and the shading along the line denotes the range of (2:   ) from a smooth curve. The shading in the right section represents the range of model projections for the IPCC scenario for the 21st century, (3:   ) to the 1980 to 1999 mean, and has been calculated independently from the observations. Over many centuries or millennia, sea level could rise by several meters.

(Source: https://wg1.ipcc.ch/publications/wg1-ar4/faq/wg1_faq-5.1.html)

a. variations   b. relative   c. estimated

80

Lots and Lots of Lithium

リチウム・ラッシュ

携帯電話や電気自動車の動力として、現代社会を支えるリチウムイオン電池。2019年ノーベル化学賞は、その開発者に授与されました。最近、豊かなリチウム鉱床と目される場所がポルトガルで新たに発見され、一獲千金をねらう企業が殺到しつつあります。この"ラッシュ"は、国家の経済戦略を左右するかもしれません。

VOCABULARY

🎧 CD 2-26

A 次の語句に対応する日本語を選びましょう。

1. prospect （　　）
2. feasible （　　）
3. reserve （　　）
4. criterion （　　）
5. extract （　　）

a. 基準
b. （鉱石を）試掘する
c. 埋蔵量
d. 実現可能な
e. 採取する

B 次の語句の下線部と同じ発音が含まれる語を、Aの語句から1つずつ選びましょう。

1. spodum<u>e</u>ne 「リシア輝石」（リチウムとアルミニウムを含むケイ酸塩鉱物の一種） （　　）

2. lithium dep<u>o</u>sits 「リチウム鉱床」 （　　）

3. m<u>i</u>ning exploration 「探鉱」 （　　）

FINDING THE TOPIC

💻 WEB動画 🎧 DVD

次の英文が映像の内容と合っている場合はTを、合っていない場合はFを選びましょう。

1. Portugal has larger lithium deposits than any other European country.　T / F

2. The results of an environmental study have just been released.　T / F

3. Portugal is expecting a lot of customers for its supplies of lithium.　T / F

CHECKING THE SCRIPT

WEB動画 🖥 DVD 💿 2-27

A 音声を聴いて、空所に入る語を書き取りましょう。
B スクリプトを読んで、内容を把握しましょう。

David Archer: CEO Savannah Resources

Fernando Queiroga: mayor of Boticas

Jorge Seguro Sanches: Portugal's Secretary of State for Energy

Narrator: David Archer knows these small dirt roads near the Portuguese town of Boticas like the back of his hand. Ever since lithium was discovered in the country's north, Archer, the head of Savannah mining company, has been ¹( ). 5 Over the last 12 months, more than 140 holes have been drilled.

David Archer: We think that Mina do Barroso is probably one of the most significant lithi…spodumene lithium ²( ) in…in Europe, 10 and it certainly sort of…could play a significant role in terms of being a keystone feature of the development of the lithium industry in…in Portugal.

Narrator: Portugal boasts Europe's largest 15 ³( ) of the silvery white metal. And Savannah estimates more than 15 to 20 million tons can be ⁴( ). Lithium is used to make batteries for mobile phones and laptops, so it's a real economic boon for the country, but the 20 environmental impact remains uncertain.

Fernando Queiroga: Of course, we don't want to hinder the progression of this project, but we are waiting for the result of the environmental study. This is really what will tell us what to expect from this 25 ⁵( ) in particular, with regard to possible environmental risks. This is our big

know…like the back of one's hand ～を熟知している
dirt road 砂利道
Boticas ボチカス（ポルトガル北部の自治体）
Savannah mining company 採掘会社のサバンナ社

in terms of… ～からすれば
keystone feature 目玉

white metal 白色合金
laptop ノート型パソコン
economic boon 経済的利益
hinder 妨げる

with regard to… ～に関して

82

concern.

Narrator: At the ministry of energy, the PR campaign for lithium mining is ready to be rolled out. 30

roll out... 〜を展開する

Campaign video: If you are an investor and you wish to find a mining ⁶( ) project, search no more! Portugal has good potential to generate good mining lithium operations with a highly competitive return ratio. 35

return ratio 還元率

Jorge Seguro Sanches: We want to impose, as criterion for the granting of licenses, the ⁷( ) of an economic development project for the region, for the country, based on what resources exist here. That is really the primary objective. 40

impose 課す
grant 認可する
drive up... 〜に拍車をかける
gear up for... 〜に備えて準備する
promising 幸先良い
nascent industry 産声を上げた産業

Narrator: As booming electric car sales drive up demand for lithium worldwide, Portugal is gearing up for the rush on the new white gold. More than half of all recent prospecting applications have been for lithium — a promising start to the nascent industry. 45

● *COMPREHENSION*

1 については質問に対する答えを、2 については下線部に入るものを選びましょう。

1. According to the video clip, which product is NOT creating demand for lithium?
   (A) Laptop computers
   (B) Electric cars
   (C) Microwave ovens
   (D) Mobile phones

2. One important _____ for granting a prospecting license is that the project should help develop the region economically.
   (A) concept   (B) contact   (C) criterion   (D) criticism

次の英文は、スクリプトの要点をプレゼンテーションのスピーチ形式にまとめたものです。
音声を聴いて、空所に入る語句を記入しましょう。

Let me first outline my presentation on developments in lithium mining.
A mining company believes that an area of Portugal has one of the most
1)_____ lithium deposits in Europe and could play a major
role in developing the lithium industry in the country. Portugal has
Europe's 2)_____ deposits of lithium, which is used to make
batteries for mobile phones, laptops, and electric cars. Portugal's ministry
of energy will soon roll out a campaign for lithium mining. As a criterion to
3)_____ licenses, the ministry wants to impose the feasibility
of an economic development project for the region and the country.
4)_____ demand for lithium is growing as a result of booming
electric car sales, and Portugal is preparing for a rush on the material.

PINPOINT

同格は、先行情報を手際よく説明する簡便な手段です。多くの場合、先行情報との間にコンマ
(,) を置きます。

> (例) Since then, Archer, the head of Savannah mining company, has been
> prospecting.
> 「それ以来、採掘会社サバンナ社の社長であるアーチャーは試掘してきました。」

英文の空所に入る適切なものを下記から選びましょう。

1. One of the most significant lithium deposits in Europe is located near Boticas,
   _____.

2. Lithium, _____, is much in demand across the globe.

3. Jorge Seguro Sanches, _____, was in charge of the PR campaign for
   lithium mining.

> a. Portugal's former energy minister
>
> b. a small municipality in northern Portugal
>
> c. one of the major materials used to make batteries

FURTHER INVESTIGATION

表 (table) やグラフ (graph) を用いずに、文章で情報を明確に表現するには、句読記号 (punctuation marks) を正しく使用することが有効です。特に、情報の列挙に便利な「:」コロン (colon) と「;」セミコロン (semicolon) の使用法に注意しましょう。

次の地図と英文は、アメリカ地質調査所 (U.S. Geological Survey [USGS]) が世界のリチウム埋蔵量について年次調査結果をまとめたものです。下記の 1 ～ 4 の (　　) 内に該当する方を選択肢から選びましょう。

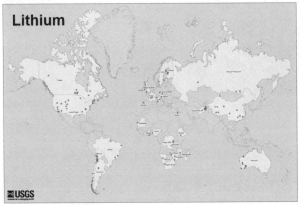

(https://mrdata.usgs.gov/pp1802/PP1802_Global.mp4)

World Resources: Owing to continuing exploration, identified lithium resources have increased substantially worldwide and total about 80 million tons. Lithium resources in the United States are 6.8 million tons. Lithium resources in other countries have been revised to 73 million tons. Lithium resources, in descending order, are: Bolivia, 21 million tons; Argentina, 17 million tons; Chile, 9 million tons; Australia, 6.3 million tons; China, 4.5 million tons; Congo, 3 million tons; Germany, 2.5 million tons; Canada and Mexico, 1.7 million tons each; Czechia, 1.3 million tons; Mali, Russia, and Serbia, 1 million tons each; Zimbabwe, 540,000 tons; Brazil, 400,000 tons; Spain, 300,000 tons; Portugal, 250,000 tons; Peru, 130,000 tons; Austria, Finland and Kazakhstan, 50,000 tons each; and Namibia, 9,000 tons.

(Source: https://pubs.usgs.gov/periodicals/mcs2020/mcs2020-lithium.pdf)

1. 確認されている世界のリチウム埋蔵量は、(増加 / 減少)している。

2. ボリビアからナミビアまでは、埋蔵量が(多い / 少ない)順に情報が整理してある。

3. カナダとメキシコの埋蔵量は、(おおむね等しい / 同じではない)。

4. ポルトガルの埋蔵量は、(30万トン / 25万トン)である。

High-tech Telescope, Low-tech Environment

18 UNIT

宇宙を感じる前線基地

電波望遠鏡の役割は、宇宙からの微細な電波をとらえること。その理想的環境は、余計な波動が一切存在しないことです。世界最大の電波望遠鏡がある米国グリーンバンクでは、電磁波を発生する機器の使用が禁止されています。現代人には一見不自由な生活のようですが、逆にそれを好む人々も確かに存在しています。

VOCABULARY

2-30

A 次の語句に対応する日本語を選びましょう。

1. energy wave　　　（　　）　　　a.　低周波
2. sensitive　　　　（　　）　　　b.　最先端の
3. jeopardy　　　　（　　）　　　c.　精度が高い、敏感な
4. low frequency　　（　　）　　　d.　エネルギー波
5. cutting-edge　　（　　）　　　e.　危険

B 次の語句の下線部と同じ発音が含まれる語を、Aの語句から1つずつ選びましょう。

1. radio telesc<u>o</u>pe　「電波望遠鏡」　　　　　　　　　　　　　　（　　）

2. interstellar d<u>u</u>st or molecule　「星間塵や星間分子」　　　　（　　）
　（星と星の間に密度の低い状態で存在する固体粒子や分子）

3. electromagnetic radi<u>a</u>tion　「電磁放射」　　　　　　　　　（　　）

FINDING THE TOPIC

WEB動画 / DVD

次の英文が映像の内容と合っている場合はTを、合っていない場合はFを選びましょう。

1. It is not only U.S. scientists that use the telescope at Green Bank.　　　T / F

2. The telescope can be used only for a limited range of observations.　　　T / F

3. Most local people feel frustrated by the limitations imposed on their
   use of electronic devices.　　　T / F

CHECKING THE SCRIPT

 2-31

A 音声を聴いて、空所に入る語を書き取りましょう。
B スクリプトを読んで、内容を把握しましょう。

Jay Lockman: lead scientist at Green Bank Observatory

Gregory Sheets: carpenter's assistant

Diane Schou: electrosensitive

Narrator: In this rural enclave that eschews modern technology, cutting-¹(   ) space research is being conducted. The rolling hills of West Virginia are home to the world's largest fully steerable radio telescope that can track and ₅ read energy ²(   ) from outer space. Scientists from around the globe vie for time using the telescope to uncover the mysteries of the universe.

enclave 飛び地
eschew 抑える
rolling hills ゆるやかな丘
陵地帯
West Virginia ウェストバー
ジニア州
be home to... ～の本拠地
である
steerable 可動型の
track 追跡する
vie for...～を奪い合う
pulsar パルサー

Jay Lockman: And if we're looking at low ³(   ), ₁₀ say, near the FM band, there we might be looking at pulsars. Whereas a factor of a thousand higher where the wavelengths are just millimeters long, there we might be looking at ⁴(   ) dust or molecules or places, clouds that are ₁₅ forming stars. So, we really have a broad range of science that's done here. And that telescope, for many, many areas of research, is the most sensitive anywhere in the world.

Narrator: Due to the sensitivity of the radio telescope, people ₂₀ in the area surrounding Green Bank can't use devices that emit a high amount of electromagnetic ⁵(   ). Chuck patrols the community to check for WiFi routers, mobile phones, and even microwaves that may be harmful ₂₅ to the telescope's research. But most locals are quite happy being low-tech.

You are Entering the Radio Astronomy Instrument Zone
• Diesel Vehicles Only

emit 放出する

87

Gregory Sheets: I don't miss the cellphone one bit. I prefer not to be called if I'm out — only if it's an emergency. They can call the house phone and leave a message, 30 and we'll get back with them.

Narrator: And the 13,000-square-mile National Radio Quiet Zone has attracted additional residents to the area — people like Diane, who suffer from electromagnetic ⁶( ), a condition not currently 35 recognized by the medical community.

National Radio Quiet Zone
ナショナル・レディオ・ク
ワイエット・ゾーン（電波の
送信が法律で制限される不
感地帯）

Diane Schou: Green Bank, not perfect, but for me it was safer than other places, and so I decided that it had to be here. And I can at least go out and see the sun, I can see the stars. Here I can live as an almost normal 40 person.

Narrator: The observatory's main source of funding has dropped by a third, which could put both future scientific discoveries and local residents' escape from modern life in ⁷( ). 45

COMPREHENSION

1 については質問に対する答えを、2 については下線部に入るものを選びましょう。

1. What is one factor that threatens the future of the Green Bank Observatory?
   (A) Its remote location
   (B) Financial problems
   (C) Dissatisfaction of local residents
   (D) The condition known as electromagnetic sensitivity

2. People are not allowed to use devices that _____ a high level of electromagnetic radiation.
   (A) transmit
   (B) remit
   (C) emit
   (D) omit

PRESENTING THE CONTENTS

2-32

次の英文は、スクリプトの要点をプレゼンテーションのスピーチ形式にまとめたものです。
音声を聴いて、空所に入る語句を記入しましょう。

The world's largest fully 1)_____ radio telescope is located in a rural area of West Virginia. Scientists come here from all over the world. The telescope enables a 2)_____ range of science to be conducted, and for many areas of research, it is the most sensitive in the world. The telescope is so sensitive that local people cannot use devices that emit a high amount of electromagnetic radiation such as WiFi routers and mobile phones. The area has also attracted residents who suffer from electromagnetic sensitivity. However, since not much data is available on this subject, the condition is not currently 3)_____ by the medical community. One problem is that the observatory's main source of 4)_____ has dropped by a third, which could threaten future scientific discoveries.

PINPOINT

「数値＋名詞 / 単位（＋形容詞)」は、文中の使用位置によって次のような違いがあります。

・名詞の前で限定形容詞的に使われる場合：ハイフンで結ばれ、名詞/単位は単数
　　The 13,000-square-mile zone is located in the east of West Virginia.

・叙述形容詞の前で副詞的に使われる場合：ハイフンは使わず、名詞/単位は複数
　　The zone located in the east of West Virginia is 13,000 square miles large.

次の英文がほぼ同じ内容になるように書きかえましょう。

1. The reflector of the Green Bank Telescope is 100 meters in diameter.

   → The Green Bank Telescope has a _____ diameter reflector.

2. The Green Bank Observatory has a more than 60-year-long observation history.

   → The observation history at the Green Bank Observatory is more than _____ _____.

FURTHER INVESTIGATION

FAQ（frequently asked questions）は、頻繁に質問される（とあらかじめ予想される）内容を、端的な Q&A 形式の一覧にまとめたものです。

次の FAQ は、NASA が計画している新たな宇宙望遠鏡 James Webb Space Telescope に関するものです。それぞれの回答（A）に対応する質問（Q）を下記から選びましょう。

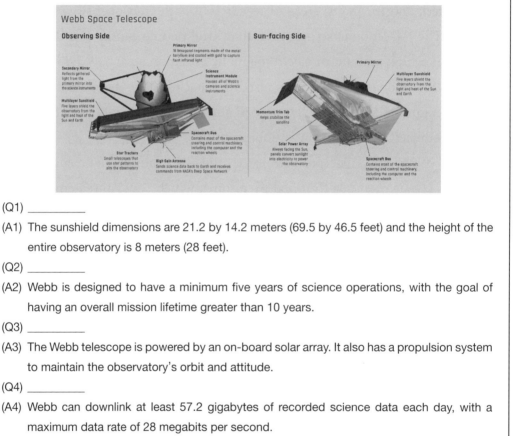

(Q1) _____

(A1) The sunshield dimensions are 21.2 by 14.2 meters (69.5 by 46.5 feet) and the height of the entire observatory is 8 meters (28 feet).

(Q2) _____

(A2) Webb is designed to have a minimum five years of science operations, with the goal of having an overall mission lifetime greater than 10 years.

(Q3) _____

(A3) The Webb telescope is powered by an on-board solar array. It also has a propulsion system to maintain the observatory's orbit and attitude.

(Q4) _____

(A4) Webb can downlink at least 57.2 gigabytes of recorded science data each day, with a maximum data rate of 28 megabits per second.

(Q5) _____

(A5) Over the course of six months, as Webb orbits the Sun with the Earth, it has the ability to observe any point in the sky.

(Based on: https://webbtelescope.org/quick-facts/telescope-quick-facts)

a. How is Webb powered?

b. What is the expected lifespan of the Webb telescope?

c. How much of the sky can Webb see?

d. How big is the Webb telescope?

e. How much data will Webb transmit each day?

Monitoring the Melting Ice

19

UNIT

気候変動の野外ラボ

南アメリカ大陸パタゴニアにあるサンタ・イネス島は、年間を通じて激しい風雨や低温にさいなまれる孤絶の地。ダイナミックな自然環境に集う多様な海洋生物の宝庫です。氷河の融解水が流れ込む海に仕掛けられたセンサーは、温暖化による海水の変化を観測しつつ、尊い生き物の豊かな営みを静かに見守っています。

VOCABULARY

CD 2-34

A 次の語句に対応する日本語を選びましょう。

1. zooplankton　　　　（　　）
2. food chain　　　　　（　　）
3. retreat　　　　　　　（　　）
4. water composition　（　　）
5. ecosystem　　　　　（　　）

a. 生態系
b. 動物性プランクトン
c. 水組成
d. 後退する
e. 食物連鎖

B 次の語句の下線部と同じ発音が含まれる語を、A の語句から 1 つずつ選びましょう。

1. the S<u>a</u>nta Ines glacier 「サンタ・イネス氷河」
   （南アメリカ最南部にあるチリ領サンタ・イネス島の氷河）　　　　　　　　　（　　）

2. micro alg<u>ae</u> 「微細藻類」　　　　　　　　　　　　　　　　　　　　　（　　）

3. conserv<u>a</u>tion plan 「（自然・文化遺産等の）保護計画」　　　　　　　　（　　）

FINDING THE TOPIC

WEB動画　DVD

次の英文が映像の内容と合っている場合は T を、合っていない場合は F を選びましょう。

1. The Santa Ines glacier is not as big as it used to be.　　　　　　　　T / F

2. The researchers obtained valuable environmental information from a　T / F
   whale that they caught.

3. Areas near the earth's poles are less likely to be affected by climate　T / F
   changes than other areas.

91

CHECKING THE SCRIPT

A 音声を聴いて、空所に入る語を書き取りましょう。
B スクリプトを読んで、内容を把握しましょう。

Marco Antonio Pinto: marine biologist, PhD student in Aquaculture Sciences from University of Chile

Maximiliano Vergara: marine biologist, PhD student in Aquaculture Sciences from University of Chile

Maximo Frangopulos Rivera: researcher at the Research Center Dynamics of High Latitude Marine Ecosystems (IDEAL)

Narrator: The humpback whale, a sea giant weighing 30 tonnes, travels thousands of kilometres to feed here, near the Santa Ines glacier, in the fjords of the Chilean Patagonia. But climate change could upset its life cycle. The glacier is ¹( ), 5 revealing rocks that were once invisible and spilling vast amounts of freshwater into the ocean. This could have serious consequences for whales, because if water ²( ) changes, it could harm their food supply. 10

humpback whale ザトウクジラ
fjords フィヨルド
upset 乱す

Marco Antonio Pinto: A modification within the micro ³( ) could generate changes in the secondary structure or in the animals that feed on it. Normally, the more micro algae there are, the more the zooplankton, which feeds on the micro 15 algae, will be able to feed and transmit this energy to higher levels in the food ⁴( ), such as to whales, dolphins or sea lions that live in the area.

the Strait of Magellan マゼラン海峡

Narrator: After two days of sailing through the Strait 20 of Magellan, this group of researchers arrive at the foot of the glacier to recover this buoy, which has been immersed for eight months. The sensors hanging from it, 10 metres deep, have recorded valuable information on the water, such 25 as temperature and acidity. These data allows

buoy ブイ（係船や航路標識のための浮標）
immerse 沈める
acidity 酸性度

[→ allow] them to closely monitor changes in the
⁵(   ).

Maximiliano Vergara: This, per se, is like nature's own unique
experiment. This allows us, without having 30
to do laboratory experiments, just by taking
measurements, to know what would happen in
similar conditions, without having to imagine it.

Narrator: As the planet warms, areas close to the poles
are particularly vulnerable to climate change. 35
Researchers say that understanding what's
happening in the sea around Patagonia could give
them a "glimpse into the future", helping them
predict how climate change will affect other places
by the end of the century. 40

Maximo Frangopulos Rivera: High-latitude waters, whether in the
northern or southern hemisphere, contain a large
amount of environmental information that could
serve as a basis for making important decisions
about the conservation ⁶(   ) of 45
developed countries and of all countries in general.

high-latitude water 高い緯度
付近の海水
northern (southern) hemi-
sphere 北（南）半球

Narrator: In the meantime, the sensor is put back into the
water, to watch over the melting
⁷(   ), and the ocean's gentle
giants. 50

in the meantime こうしてい
るうちに

watch over 見守る

◖COMPREHENSION

1 については質問に対する答えを、2 については下線部に入るものを選びましょう。

1. Why are the researchers working near the Santa Ines glacier in Patagonia?
   (A) It is the only area where humpback whales can be found.
   (B) Areas near the poles provide them with valuable information.
   (C) That area is warming faster than other areas on the earth.
   (D) There is a nearby laboratory for performing experiments.

2. Analysis of the data could give the researchers a _____ into the future.
   (A) knowledge   (B) survey   (C) glimpse   (D) dream

次の英文は、スクリプトの要点をプレゼンテーションのスピーチ形式にまとめたものです。音声を聴いて、空所に入る語句を記入しましょう。

I'd like to demonstrate how climate change threatens the life 1)_____ of humpback whales. These animals come to the fjords of Patagonia to feed, but a recent study showed that the melting of a glacier is spilling a vast amount of freshwater into the ocean. If this changes the water composition, it could harm the whales' food 2)_____. Researchers collected a buoy containing sensors, which recorded valuable information on the water, such as temperature and acidity. These data allow them to closely 3)_____ changes in the ecosystem without using laboratory experiments. Because areas near the earth's poles are particularly 4)_____ to climate change, this information could help the researchers predict how climate change will affect other places, which will help people to make important decisions.

● *PINPOINT*

動詞を利用して「重量」「寸法・面積」「収容人数」などを表現する構文には、次のようなものがあります。

・主語 + weigh + X「主語の重さはXである」
・主語 + measure + X「主語（の寸法・面積）はXである」
  cf. 主語＋measure the temperature / length of X「主語はXの温度/長さを測る」
・主語 + accommodate + X「主語の収容人数はXである」

英文の空所に入る適切な語を下記から選びましょう。

1. The area of Santa Ines Island _____ 3,688 square kilometres.

2. The research vessel _____ up to 50 crew members.

3. The iceberg observed near Antarctica presumably _____ about one trillion tonnes.

accommodates   weighed   measures

FURTHER INVESTIGATION

> 分布図（distribution map）は、ある事象の分布状況を地図上の色分けや濃淡によって示すものです。

次の枠内は、南極大陸に存在する氷河の流動速度を示す新たな分布図と、その公開を紹介した記事です。下記の1〜4から、分布図や英文の内容と合っているものを2つ選びましょう。

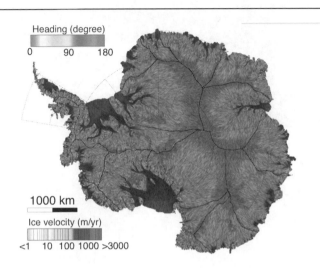

Far more accurate than any previous map, this new representation of glacier flows in Antarctica opens the door to an improved understanding of the vast continent and the future pace of sea level rise. All earlier maps of glacier flow speeds have estimated the speeds largely by tracking the movement of visible features like patches of dirt on the ice surface, but these new maps rely mainly on observations that use a technique called synthetic aperture radar interferometry, which is much more sensitive to the motion of the ice itself. By combining observations from multiple satellites passing over the continent in different directions, the researchers produced a map that is not only 10 times more accurate than any previous map but also shows speeds for far more of the slow-moving ice on the continental interior than ever before.

(Source: https://climate.nasa.gov/news/2897/flowing-antarctic-ice-mapped-10-times-more-accurately/)

1.　この新しい分布図は、将来的な海水面上昇に関する理解を促進する可能性がある。

2.　従来の同種の分布図は、複数の人工衛星による観測データを組み合わせて作成していた。

3.　この新しい分布図では、流動速度が遅い氷河の情報が従来の分布図よりも多く得られる。

4.　流動速度が速い氷河が比較的多く存在するのは、地図上の右側である。

Creating Mars in the Desert

20
UNIT

砂漠から見上げる赤い星

火星への移住。世界の人口爆発や小惑星と地球の衝突予測などを背景に、近年、その可能性が真面目に論議されています。疑似火星環境での生存実験も熱を帯び、あるプロジェクトが選んだ拠点は中東・オマーンの砂漠。かつて古代の天文学が発達した灼熱の地は、現在も宇宙への "ゲートウェイ" となっています。

VOCABULARY

CD 2-38

A 次の語句に対応する日本語を選びましょう。

1.	resource	( )	a.	小惑星
2.	stem from…	( )	b.	〜に由来する
3.	sustain	( )	c.	絞めつける、制限する
4.	asteroid	( )	d.	資源
5.	constrict	( )	e.	維持する

B 次の語句の下線部と同じ発音が含まれる語を、A の語句から 1 つずつ選びましょう。

1. pressure-simulating suit「気圧実験スーツ」 ( )

2. Austrian Space Forum (= OeWF)「オーストリア宇宙フォーラム」 ( )

3. AMADEE-18 Mars Analog Mission「AMADEE-18火星模擬ミッション」
   （OeWFによる国際的な火星疑似実験） ( )

FINDING THE TOPIC

WEB動画
DVD

次の英文が映像の内容と合っている場合は T を、合っていない場合は F を選びましょう。

1. The training for Mars was set up jointly by the government of Oman and the Australian Space Forum. T / F

2. On Mars, astronauts will not be able to move as easily as they do on earth. T / F

3. The US has declared that it will start mining on Mars one day in the future. T / F

● *CHECKING THE SCRIPT*

A 音声を聴いて、空所に入る語を書き取りましょう。
B スクリプトを読んで、内容を把握しましょう。

Alexander Soucek: President of the Austrian Space Forum and AMADEE-18 flight director on earth

Joao Lousada: test astronaut and volunteer researcher

Narrator: It may look like a scene from a science fiction movie, but these astronauts clad in ¹( )-simulating suits have their feet firmly on earth — in Oman's barren desert, more specifically. They're taking part in simulation 5 training, aiming to one day help humans survive on Mars.

science fiction movie
SF映画
clad in... 〜を着た
have one's feet on...
〜に足をつける
barren 不毛な
most of all とりわけ
operationally 任務遂行
に際して

Alexander Soucek: We need a place that looks as much like Mars as possible. And we found it here in Oman, it's a beautiful place, but it's most of all a scientifically 10 useful place and operationally useful place.

Narrator: Run by the Austrian Space Forum with backing from the Omani government, the AMADEE-18 Mars ²( ) Mission brings together researchers, inventors, space professionals 15 and enthusiasts — all with their sights set on the red planet. In early February, US billionaire Elon Musk launched the world's most powerful rocket towards an orbit near Mars. In this remote corner of the Arabian Peninsula, the European-led project 20 is far less flashy, but still looks to answer major questions.

enthusiast 熱狂的ファン

the red planet 火星
billionaire 億万長者
launch 発射する

orbit 軌道

Arabian Peninsula
アラビア半島
flashy 目立つ

Alexander Soucek: Once we will go to Mars and we will stay on Mars, we will have to use the ³( ) we find on Mars because we cannot bring everything 25 from earth. So, we have to use the things we find there, first of all to ⁴( ) life there,

to sustain missions there, and then in the longer run, maybe, also for other things.

Narrator: Everything is custom-built to resemble the ⁵(   ) movement astronauts would feel on Mars. Along with the training, the team have reflected on other issues ⁶(   ) from space exploration. Since 2015, the US and Luxembourg have been creating legal frameworks that could eventually allow mining in space. The EU has yet to take a position on the controversial topic.

Joao Lousada: Mining comes into a bit of a legal loophole where it's not clear for all organisations whether it is legally feasible or not. I think definitely we should look into using resources that we can maybe gather from ⁷(   ), that are not available on earth, or not as frequent on earth.

Narrator: Meanwhile, these volunteer researchers are set to explore the Omani desert, looking to set foot on the coveted red planet and turn science fiction into reality.

30

35

40

45

in the longer run
より長期的には

custom-built 特注の

space exploration
宇宙探査
legal framework
法的な体制
EU (= European Union)
欧州連合
have yet to... まだ～して
いない
controversial 議論を呼ぶ

loophole 抜け穴
feasible 実行可能な
independent of... ～は
別にして
be set to... ～することにな
っている
look to... ～をめざす
coveted 切望される

● COMPREHENSION

1 については質問に対する答えを、2 については下線部に入るものを選びましょう。

1. What is the main purpose of the operation in the Omani desert?
   (A) To train astronauts for various space missions
   (B) To teach people how to survive on Mars
   (C) To study mining techniques that could be used in space
   (D) To help US billionaire Elon Musk with his research

2. The astronauts are taking _____ in simulation training in the desert.
   (A) place   (B) part   (C) up   (D) over

🔵 *PRESENTING THE CONTENTS*   🎧 2-40

次の英文は、スクリプトの要点をプレゼンテーションのスピーチ形式にまとめたものです。
音声を聴いて、空所に入る語句を記入しましょう。

Today, I will address the topic of space exploration: more precisely, not
space exploration itself but the training necessary for it. In the deserts of
Oman, simulation training is underway aimed at helping humans one
day to 1)_____ on Mars. The Austrian Space Forum, which
runs the training, views conditions in Oman's deserts as somewhat close
to those on Mars. The project has gathered researchers, inventors, and
space professionals. Such training is essential because astronauts going to
Mars will have to rely on the 2)_____ they find there, as it will
be impossible to bring everything necessary from Earth. All the training
equipment is 3)_____ to resemble the constricted movement
that astronauts would feel on Mars. One day, perhaps, the volunteers in the
desert will turn science fiction into 4)_____.

🔵 *PINPOINT*

過去形の助動詞（"would" "might" など）は、しばしば「現在」の時点で断定を避ける場合
に効果的に使用されます。

（例）Legal frameworks between the nations could eventually allow mining in
space.
「国家間の法的な体制が、やがて宇宙での採鉱を許容することもありえるだろう。」

日本語を参考にして、［ ］内の語句を適切な語順に並べかえましょう。

1. Billionaires like Elon Musk _____ toward
   Mars in the future.

   [manned / would / rockets / launch]
   「イーロン・マスクのような億万長者が、将来火星に有人ロケットを打ち上げるかもしれない。」

2. With technologies developed to utilise the resources on Mars, _____
   _____.

   [there / could / survive / humans]
   「火星にある資源を利用するための技術が進歩すれば、人類はそこで生きのびることができるかもしれな
   い。」

● *FURTHER INVESTIGATION*

> NASA の宇宙服には、材料や機能、構造などの面で、やがて我々の身の回りの製品に応用される先端技術が豊富に用いられています。

次の写真は NASA で使用されている宇宙服のパーツです。それぞれの説明を選びましょう。

1. (　　　)　　　　　　2. (　　　)　　　　　　3. (　　　)

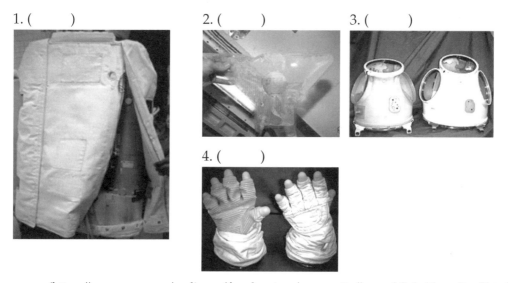

4. (　　　)

(https://www.nasa.gov/audience/foreducators/spacesuits/home/clickable_suit_nf.html)

a. **Hard Upper Torso**: The HUT covers the chest and back. It is a vest made out of fiberglass like some cars and swimming pools. An important function of this piece is that it serves as the connection for the tubes that drain water and allow oxygen flow.

b. **EVA Gloves**: Astronauts must be able to work with and pick up objects while wearing spacesuit gloves. They are made so spacewalkers can move their fingers as easily as possible. The fingers are the part of the body that gets coldest in space. These gloves have heaters in the fingertips.

c. **Primary Life Support Subsystem**: The PLSS is worn like a backpack. It provides astronauts many of the things they need to survive on a spacewalk. Its tanks supply oxygen for the astronauts to breathe. It removes exhaled carbon dioxide. It contains a battery for electrical power.

d. **In-Suit Drink Bag**: A plastic, water-filled pouch attaches to the inside of the Hard Upper Torso using Velcro. A plastic tube with a valve sticks out of the bag. Biting the valve opens the tube so the spacewalker can take a drink.

リンガポルタ連動テキストをご購入の学生さんは、「リンガポルタ」を無料でご利用いただけます！

本テキストで学習していただく内容に準拠した問題を、オンライン学習システム「リンガポルタ」で学習していただくことができます。PCだけでなく、スマートフォンやタブレットでも学習できます。単語や文法、リスニング力などをよりしっかり身に付けていただくため、ぜひ積極的に活用してください。

リンガポルタの利用にはアカウントとアクセスコードの登録が必要です。登録方法については下記ページにアクセスしてください。

https://www.seibido.co.jp/linguaporta/register.html

本テキスト「AFP SciTech Futures」のアクセスコードは下記です。

7231-2045-1231-0365-0003-006b-21WE-EC8S

・リンガポルタの学習機能（画像はサンプルです。また、すべてのテキストに以下の4つの機能が用意されているわけではありません）

多肢選択

空所補充（音声を使っての聞き取り問題も可能）

単語並びかえ（マウスや手で単語を移動）

マッチング（マウスや手で単語を移動）

Web動画のご案内　**StreamLine**

本テキストの映像は、オンラインでのストリーミング再生になります。下記URLよりご利用ください。なお**有効期限は、はじめてログインした時点から1年半**です。

http://st.seibido.co.jp

ログイン画面

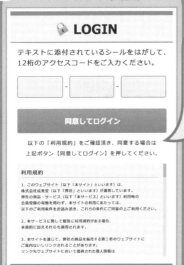

> 巻末に添付されているシールをはがして、アクセスコードをご入力ください。

メニュー画面

> 「Video」または「Audio」を選択すると、それぞれストリーミング再生ができます。

再生画面

推奨動作環境

【PC OS】
Windows 7～ ／ Mac 10.8～

【Mobile OS】
iOS ／ Android ※Android の場合は4.x～が推奨

【Desktop ブラウザ】
Internet Explorer 9～ / Firefox / Chrome / Safari / Microsoft Edge

TEXT PRODUCTION STAFF

edited by	編集
Takashi Kudo	工藤 隆志

cover design by	表紙デザイン
Nobuyoshi Fujino	藤野 伸芳

text design by	本文デザイン
Ruben Frosali	ルーベ ン・フロサリ

CD PRODUCTION STAFF

recorded by	吹き込み者
Howard Colefield (AmE)	ハワード・コールフィルド（アメリカ英語）
Jennifer Okano (AmE)	ジェニファー・オカノ（アメリカ英語）
Karen Haedrich (AmE)	カレン・ヘドリック（アメリカ英語）
Neil DeMaere (AmE)	ニール・デマル（アメリカ英語）

AFP SciTech Futures
AFPで学ぶ世界の科学

2021年1月10日	初版発行
2024年3月20日	第7刷発行

著　者	椋平 淳　　Bill Benfield　　辻本 智子
	大塚 生子　藏薗 和也　　瀧川 宏樹
	湯浅 麻里子　松本 敬子

発 行 者　　佐野 英一郎

発 行 所　　株式会社 成 美 堂
　　　　　　〒101-0052　東京都千代田区神田小川町3-22
　　　　　　TEL 03-3291-2261　FAX 03-3293-5490
　　　　　　https://www.seibido.co.jp

印 刷・製 本　　倉敷印刷株式会社

ISBN 978-4-7919-7231-9　　　　　　　　　　Printed in Japan